The Afterlife Connection

My mother Helen and I on vacation in Italy.

The Afterlife Connection

A Therapist Reveals How to Communicate with Departed Loved Ones

DR. JANE GREER

ST. MARTIN'S GRIFFIN ≈ NEW YORK

www.stmartins.com

Library of Congress Cataloging-in-Publication Data

Greer, Jane, 1951–
    The afterlife connection : a therapist reveals how to communicate with departed loved ones / Jane Greer.
        p. cm.
    ISBN 0-312-30652-0 (hc)
    ISBN 0-312-30653-9 (pbk)
    EAN 978-0312-30653-3
    1. Spiritualism. I. Title.

BF1261.2.G74 2003
133.9—dc21   2003047146

10 9 8 7 6 5 4 3

To my father

For your unconditional love throughout my life.

When it counts the most, you're always there.

I love you.

Life is eternal,
Love is immortal,
And death is only a horizon . . .
And the horizon is nothing
Save the limit of our sight.

—CARLY SIMON, "Life Is Eternal"

Contents

Introduction
My Mother's Promise

The angels, whispering to one another, can find amid their burning terms of love, none so devotional as that of "Mother."

—EDGAR ALLAN POE

It's more than four years ago as of this writing that my mother, Helen, and I were chatting and laughing as we crossed Madison Avenue. She'd come up to New York from Florida, where she and my father lived, and we'd spent the morning shopping and just enjoying one another's company. It was one of those wonderful September days when the weather is still balmy and the sky a cloudless, clear blue. The only thing that made it less than perfect was the fact that my mother, who never complained about physical problems, was complaining that she had a splitting headache. I thought she probably needed new glasses and suggested that when she got back home, she make an appointment with the eye doctor.

I remember walking my dogs one day just a week or so before she arrived and thinking how lucky I was that both my parents had so much longevity in their families. My mother's mother had lived to ninety-four and her mother's sister, my great aunt, to ninety-three. I thought I'd certainly be fortunate enough to have my mother with me for perhaps another twenty years.

Because of her family history and her own good health, as well as the fact that she practiced yoga every day, played golf regularly, and had always been extremely careful about what she ate, it never occurred to me that she could be seriously ill. Over the next few days her headache persisted, however, and again I urged her to make that eye doctor's appointment.

The following Wednesday, she went back to Florida as planned, promising that she would call the ophthalmologist. On Friday she dinged her brand-new car trying to maneuver her way out of a parking lot because, as she described the incident to my father, she couldn't see the car that was to the side of hers. My parents called me that night to report what had happened. They'd already made an emergency visit to the eye doctor, who said that my mother had lost her peripheral vision. He was concerned and had told them she needed an immediate MRI to determine the cause. The test was scheduled for Monday morning. I, too, was concerned about her vision, but because her driving stories were, and continue to be, legend in our family, I still wasn't terribly worried. I thought she might have had a mini-stroke. But my great aunt had suffered a series of mini-strokes and had nevertheless enjoyed an extremely long life. My mother was only seventy-seven. I just hoped there wouldn't be any permanent damage, and that she'd recover her vision fully and quickly.

Sunday, my mother called again. She was certain that something was terribly wrong, and she was frightened. She started to talk about the fact that she wanted to be cremated. Although I still genuinely believed she'd be fine, I responded to her fears by saying if that's what she wanted, she'd have to choose a very special place to scatter her ashes. I asked her where that would be, and we began to talk about places that were meaningful to her. Never for a minute did I consider that there could be anything seriously wrong with her. In fact, as was her typical style, she began to make jokes about which spot to choose, and we were able to laugh together even while discussing such a frightening subject.

I knew my parents would call as soon as my mother had the results of her test on Monday, so when I hadn't heard from them by four o'clock, I was getting pretty anxious. At four-thirty, my father did call. "Your mother has a brain tumor," he said. When I heard that, it was as if I'd been hit over the head with a brick. "This can't be happening," was my immediate reaction. He told me she needed immediate surgery, and that the operation had been scheduled for Wednesday morning. I told him my husband, Marc, and I would be there the next day and hung up in a complete state of shock to make plans.

From that point on, my life became surreal. It was hard for me to grasp the fact that the rest of the world was unchanged, that other people were going about their everyday business as usual. My own world had come to a grinding halt. The phrase *falling apart* took on a very personal meaning. It didn't matter where I was, both during her illness and after her death—if someone asked me how my mother was doing or offered his or her sympathy, I might suddenly burst into tears. It might even be in the middle of a therapy session. I simply couldn't prevent the upsurge of emotion. And then, at other times, I'd be perfectly able to talk rationally and reasonably about what was happening.

For the first time in my life, my feelings were completely unpredictable and totally beyond my control.

Throughout my life my mother and I had always shared so much of one another's lives that we seemed more like sisters than mother and daughter. The thought of losing her was simply unfathomable to me. She knew all of my friends and I knew hers. My friends often went with me to Florida, where we'd all spend time together, sometimes joining her friends for lunches, dinners, or a movie. To this day, her friends and I have stayed in touch, which is an ongoing connection that has been extremely heartening to me.

One loss I still feel deeply is no longer being able to share our physical resemblance. Not only did we feel like sisters, we also looked and sounded so much alike that people would routinely remark on the fact that we had "the same face." Even now, when I speak, I very often hear my mother's voice. Her style was distinctive, but sometimes we could also wear the same clothes. Even now, I might see a particular dress or outfit in a shop and think, "That's exactly my mother." Just knowing there was someone in this world whose bond to me was so genetically obvious somehow allowed me to feel that we belonged together. I felt that we were so much a part of one another that I could never truly be alone so long as my mother was in the world.

Visiting her was always a joy, no matter what we were actually doing. We might be shopping, playing cards for hours on end, discussing a movie we'd seen—her taste in movies was often more intellectual than mine—talking about a book we'd read, or gossiping about friends; it didn't matter. We talked about anything and everything. I basked in her wisdom, her wit, and her unfailing generosity of spirit.

She was an intuitive therapist who had the right words or a personal expression—which I always think of as "Helenisms"—for every moment of living. She was able to smooth the rough edges, provide me with a sense of perspective, and help me to manage in any situation. Early on, she taught me always to consider the other person's feelings. Ever tactful and caring, she told me that if I had something negative or critical to say, I should "say it euphemistically." I wasn't the only one who benefited from her unique sensibility, however. She simply had a knack for helping everyone feel special and find what was best within themselves.

She herself was a political activist who, for many years, had been the vice president of the Democratic Women of Bergen County, New Jersey. She held a series of political jobs and was also a licensed realtor. By both her example and her words, she inspired and encouraged me to persevere no matter how overwhelming or difficult a situation might seem. One of the stories she loved to tell at times when I couldn't see the light at the end of the tunnel was about the frog who fell into a bowl of cream. He was starting to drown, so he kept swimming and struggling to get out. But he kept falling back in and struggling some more. Finally, he flailed so much that the cream turned to butter, and he was able to hop out. So, she would remind me, even when the situation seems impossible, you have to just keep struggling because there's always a way out of every dilemma!

Luckily, I never had to struggle alone because I knew my mother would always be there, cheering me on, telling me, as she did whenever I had a moment of self-doubt about my ability to accomplish something or achieve a goal I'd set for myself, "You can; you will; don't worry!" She shared all of my excitement, all of my hopes, all of my schemes, and all of my dreams. She was my greatest ally, the one person who always made me believe I could take on the world.

My mother had such a sharp wit that spending time with her was like having a human funny bone at your side. It was inconceivable to me that anyone else would have, as my cousin Jonathan put it, "her goofy worldview and spirited lust for life," or would be able to make the jokes she made. We shared the silly and petty moments of our days as well as all the major events of our lives.

It was my mother's constant encouragement that kept me on my chosen career path. Without her positive reinforcement at moments when I had to make pivotal choices, I might easily have wavered or stopped short of my goal.

She was a force, and as you will see, she is now a force field to contend with. Sometimes, for my own good, she'd force me to do something I didn't want to do, and in those moments she'd tell me, with her characteristic humor, "Be reasonable; do it my way."

Learning of her illness was a shattering moment in my life, a turning point that challenged my ability to cope and shook my spiritual foundation.

Neither my mother nor I ever pretended that her brain tumor was anything other than terminal. She'd been diagnosed with a glioblastoma, which is the fastest-growing, most aggressive form of brain tumor. Treatment options are both limited and debilitating. After the operation, we all hoped her vision would return. When it didn't, and when she understood that there was no cure for her condition—the doctors had given her from six to eighteen months—she faced the inevitable with the same stoicism she'd always exhibited. She determined to stop taking the medications that were making her feel even worse and to live out her time with as much dignity as she could muster. It was a difficult choice for us to accept but one that we respected. I tried to be positive and upbeat, at least when we were together, but it wasn't always possible for me to hold back my tears or hide the utter anguish I felt when I contemplated losing her constant, unconditional love and unwavering support.

In the following months her health deteriorated to the point where even the simplest act, such as brushing her teeth, became a seemingly impossible task. She lost her strength and her mobility. Her inability to do the things that had always been so much a part of her life left her depressed. Her sense of humor, though, remained intact, and she was even able to make my father and me laugh about the things she could no longer do.

I didn't know how I'd be able to let her go, but the understanding that our time together was quickly drawing to a close forced me to contemplate what my life would be without her. Although we'd discussed the subject of psychic phenomena in a general way, and, in her usual, open-minded fashion, she'd been willing to accept the possibility, we'd never talked specifically about afterlife communication. Then, about four months before she died, I broached the subject of our ongoing communication. I had gone to Florida to visit, as I did frequently during those months, and we were in her bedroom. I was holding her hand and telling her I loved her when, suddenly overwhelmed by the certainty of her impending death, I began to cry. "Promise me that after you're gone, you'll find a way to contact me," I said. I don't know that I'd really thought about what I was going to say before the words came out of my mouth. I just desperately didn't want to lose her, and this was a way for me not to have to say a final good-bye.

She nodded, but I needed more. I needed to hear the words. "Promise me, Mom," I repeated.

Our eyes locked, and, seeing the conviction in mine, she said, "I promise."

At that moment, as we faced one another, I knew that, somehow, she would keep her word to me. At the time, however, I had no clear or fixed ideas about how it would happen.

The last time I saw my mother, she was near death but still struggling to hold on. As Marc and I were saying our final good-byes, Marc leaned toward her and said, "Helen, it's okay; you can go now." We then left for the airport.

We'd landed in New York and were in the car, on our way home, when my cell phone rang. It was my father calling to tell us my mother had died.

The following weekend, Marc and I returned to Florida to honor my mother's request that she be cremated. The morning after we arrived dawned hot, humid, and muggy. It was only the beginning of May, but summer had already arrived in South Florida. All the windows in my parents' house were shut tight, and the air conditioner had been left on low overnight. Not so much as a breeze stirred the curtains, but a family photograph that had stood for years on the breakfront in the living room had somehow toppled and now lay facedown in its frame. Instantly, I felt that my mother had been responsible for turning it over and that this was her first afterlife connection with me.

Later that day, as I entered the airport terminal, the reality of her being gone really sank in, leaving me literally numb with sorrow. This was a trip Marc and I had made countless times, but today I wouldn't be calling my mother to say we'd landed safely. Even with my husband right beside me, I felt completely lost and alone.

"I really want to feel your presence, but I can't," I said aloud to my mother.

No sooner had the words left my lips than the sliding glass terminal door slammed into my right arm. I winced, then had to laugh to myself. I'd wanted to feel something definitive, and I'd just been hit in the arm. I could certainly feel that! Of course, at that point, I told myself, I was so oblivious of my surroundings that I'd unconsciously been standing directly in front of the door, so it was certainly possible that I was fulfilling my own request. But still . . .

As a child, I was always intrigued by the potency of the mind. Although I'd never had a psychic experience of my own, the very possibility of such a phenomenon was exciting. I remember being fascinated by Rod Serling's *Twilight Zone,* and particularly by the words he spoke at the beginning of each episode.

> There is a fifth dimension beyond that which is known to man. It is a dimension as vast as space and as timeless as infinity. It is the middle ground between light and shadow, between science and superstition, and it lies between the pit of man's fears and the summit of his knowledge. . . .

In fact, when I was in fifth or sixth grade, we were given the assignment of picking a celebrity we admired and writing to him or her asking for a picture. I wrote to Rod Serling and received an autographed photo that I kept for many years. Although the show was clearly fanciful, that notion of another dimension had seized my imagination.

As a young woman, like many of my contemporaries who

wanted to know when we would meet Mr. Right, I went to see a psychic for the first time. I recall that when she mentioned my grandmother, the overhead light went out. At the time, although I was vaguely aware that it might have some significance, I didn't think very much of it—in fact I'd embarked on the whole adventure as something of a lark.

Now, however, my need to know my mother was still with me in spirit was anything but a lark. My mother's illness, and then her death, had turned the canvass of my life from vibrant Technicolor to black-and-white. It was as if I'd traveled from Oz back to Kansas.

As you'll see, the signs and signals she began to send me almost immediately following her death were undeniable. She'd already begun her ongoing communication when, two months after her passing, Marc and I were back in Florida. The air-conditioning in the guest bedroom wasn't working, so we bedded down in the living room, directly across from the urn containing her ashes. At 12:30 we turned off the light and went to sleep. Sometime later I was awakened with a start when the light went on all by itself for absolutely no reason. At first I was scared, thinking that someone might be breaking into the house. Then, all of a sudden I said to myself, "I bet it's the same time she passed." I got up and went into the kitchen to check the time. It was 2:26 A.M. I tried to go back to sleep after that but felt compelled to confirm my hunch. I went to the desk to pull out my mother's death certificate. There it was, the time of her death: 2:26. I knew, of course, that my mother had died at 2:26 in the afternoon, but beyond the boundaries of time and space, it seemed to me, such distinctions might well be less important than they are to us. In any case, the whole event felt too significant to be mere coincidence. If her energy hadn't been in the room, then what had turned on the light? I could think of no satisfactory answer to that question.

When I later told the story to my cousin Marta, she actually gasped. "What's the matter?" I asked. "Nothing's the matter," she said. "It's just so amazing! The last time I saw your mother, about a month before she was diagnosed, she brought me a little clock as a present. It wasn't working when she gave it to me, so I put in new batteries. It worked like a charm and then stopped for no reason right after she died. The amazing thing is that it stopped at exactly two-twenty-six. I didn't even know her time of death until you just mentioned it."

My father, too, had begun to have his own startling experiences. The first occurred when all four of his watches and all four of the telephones in their house—two of them brand-new—suddenly stopped working. Was there a significance to the fact that these malfunctions involved items that are used to measure time and facilitate communication? I believed then, as I do now, that my mother was communicating from that fifth dimension beyond the boundaries of time and space.

In the months and years since then, I've experienced countless phenomena—dream visits, appearances in a variety of animal forms, inexplicable mechanical malfunctions, and numerous other messages—that have convinced me of my mother's ability to keep her promise to stay in touch. I've also discovered my own ability to initiate meaningful communications with her. How to develop such an ability is what I want to share with you.

Skeptics may scoff and declare these events no more than random happenings, and that is certainly their right. Those with far keener scientific minds than mine, however, suggest that the frequency and recurring patterns of such occurrences preclude the possibility of mere coincidence. The more I've read about and investigated these sorts of afterlife communications, the more certain I've become that my ability to stay connected to my mother is not unique to me. It's not a function of any extraordinary psychic power, and it's not simply a fluke. Rather, I believe that the world of spirit is remarkably accessible to all of us. If we are just willing to open ourselves to the possibility, we can discover and cultivate a continuing connection to those important people in our lives who have passed away.

These communications have not prevented me from mourning my mother's death or from feeling the searing pain of her loss. Indeed, her passing has left me at times with almost unbearable sorrow. For almost two years I simply didn't have the energy to "dress up." As a short person who is also mindful of presenting a professional appearance, I normally wear skirts and high heels every day. Now, however, I could wear nothing but trousers and flats. Emotionally, I needed to be grounded, with my feet flat on the floor.

The knowledge that I am still connected to her energy and spirit has nevertheless helped ease the grief of her physical absence. During those first months, whenever I received a sign from her, it was as if I'd been in full-blown pain and then been given a shot of Demerol. I knew the pain was still there, but at least for the moment it was dulled to the point where I could bear it. I now understand that she will continue to be with me for as long as I live—and, perhaps, beyond the borders of my mortal existence. That understanding has had a profound impact on my own healing, as I believe it can ultimately have for you.

Professionally, it is my goal to facilitate my patients' achieving happier, more fulfilling lives. Personally, I understand and have experienced the degree to which afterlife communication can strengthen the psychological connection we all have with loved ones who die by helping us to cultivate a psychic bond as well. Now I want to share the tools I've acquired, sharpened, and polished along my journey, so that you, too, will be able to benefit from what I've learned. My hope is that you will experience the same kind of joy and relief my mother's messages have brought me.

Many of us are able to stay connected to a departed loved one by maintaining a psychological and emotional bond. We do that in various ways, depending on what feels comfortable for us. We might keep a cherished object or an article of clothing. We might remember our loved one on special occasions or in special places—by visiting the cemetery or a place where we used to spend time together, or just by sitting in a quiet corner. Talking to family and friends who also knew him or her is yet another way to bring the personality of the departed to life. In fact, we very often speak directly to our departed loved ones at times of accomplishment, when we know they would approve and be proud of us. That's why, at awards ceremonies or after winning a sporting event, we so often hear the honoree saying, "Mom, Dad, this is for you. I know you're watching." We might also light a candle, say a prayer, or hold onto a photograph. For many, keeping a plant alive becomes a way to keep alive a part of the person with whom it's associated. Even my father, who had never watered a plant in his life, began to water my mother's plants after she died. While he's watering them, he talks to her, saying, "Helen, can you believe I'm doing this? I can't believe it. You've got me watering plants." He's kept them alive for four years now. Her spirit continues to live for him through those plants.

Many of you, I'm sure, have already experienced these kinds

of emotional and psychological bonds. If you have not yet embraced the notion of the psychic or afterlife connection I'm describing, I simply encourage you to consider the possibility of expanding and deepening your bond. The very fact that you bought this book and have begun to read it must mean that, on some level, you've already taken a small leap of faith. If you already speak to your loved one, I'm suggesting that you can take it one step farther. You can learn how to initiate specific contact and then how to recognize the responses and messages you receive.

Establishing that spiritual and psychic bond can make you feel safe and protected. It can enable you to believe you have a guardian angel who will continue to watch over you, love you, and care about you. Knowing your loved one is with you, being able to feel his or her presence, will help you to transcend your anxieties, loneliness, and feelings of abandonment.

In addition, establishing that afterlife bond helps to create the understanding that you will someday be reunited with your loved one. That belief can, in itself, be incredibly empowering because it can alter and alleviate your own fear of death. It can give you hope.

While remembering your loved one in special ways will provide you with a psychological safety net, developing an afterlife connection will give you the opportunity to take your ongoing bond to a whole new dynamic, metaphysical dimension.

Part One

Discovering the
Afterlife Connection

1.

From Therapist to Soul-Searcher — My Journey Begins

Death lies on her like an untimely frost
Upon the sweetest flower of all the field.

—**WILLIAM SHAKESPEARE**, *Romeo and Juliet*

The death of a loved one inevitably changes the course of your life. For me, as a therapist, that meant using my experience as a way to help others, turning my pain into something positive, growth-promoting, and most of all healing.

As I've said, my mother's death caused a seismic upheaval in my own life. I have been a mainstream, psychoanalytically trained and certified therapist and a licensed marriage and family counselor for more than twenty years. I am also a media consultant and an author who has written standard self-help books addressing such issues as betrayal, psychological or emotional gridlock, and adult sibling rivalry. Since I'm the sex columnist for *Redbook* magazine on-line, I had planned, at the time of my mother's diagnosis, to continue my writing with a book about sexual relationships. The subject of the book you're now reading is by far the last one I would ever have thought I'd be writing about.

At first I struggled with the idea of sharing such a personal relationship. To do so goes against my most basic training as a psychotherapist, which is to avoid self-disclosure. Finally, however, I realized that my experience had taught me something really vital to the healing process—something that, in order to honor a valuable lesson I learned long ago, I needed to pass on.

Although it didn't become entirely clear to me until after my mother's death just how much psychic ability has been given to each of us, I've always had an abiding faith in the power of the mind and a desire to explore the farthest reaches of our mental abilities. It was, in fact that faith and desire that led me to become a therapist in the first place.

Twinless Twins

My doctoral dissertation involved research into the special bond that exists between both identical and fraternal twins and whether it would either negatively or positively affect their marital relationships. Most of us have heard twins talk about the psychic bond that allows them to sense one another's thoughts. We hear about twins separated at birth who, years later, discover that they've both married women named Sue or have both become doctors specializing in the same branch of medicine. There are stories of twins who, as children, communicate in a special secret language and who sometimes even refuse to communicate in their actual native language.

Many of the twins I interviewed in the course of my research spoke about the closeness of that bond, often referring to themselves as "womb mates." But I was particularly struck, when I went on to begin counseling twins who had lost their twin siblings, by their insistence that no one could understand the magnitude of their loss. In expressing it to me, they said, "It's like losing a part of yourself." The twins I encountered believed absolutely in the existence of an ongoing connection with their deceased sibling in spirit that was not simply metaphorical but as real as the bond they'd had in life. It was just that conviction that led Raymond Brandt, who had lost his identical twin sibling at the age of twenty, to found the Twinless Twins Support Group, in whose activities I had the opportunity to participate for several years, as a forum for helping twins deal with their unique loss and grief.

At the time I hadn't had any personal experience with after-death communication, but I accepted the phenomena this group was reporting as in some way very real. I understood that their unwavering sense of connection played an important part in these people's ability to survive emotionally and heal their grief. Even then, the twins' stories had a formidable impact upon me. In retrospect I've come to see that the absolute certainty of their belief had a lot to do with opening my own mind to the possibility of the soul's survival after death.

One patient, Alexis, whose twin sister, Alice, had died suddenly and tragically in a small plane crash, described the loss of her twin by saying. "It takes you to a place described by Rilke as the 'massive darkness of grief.'" Then she added, "I have seen the abyss." When I spoke to her on the phone these many years later, the grief was still palpable in her voice.

She also, however, talked about the many ongoing messages, phenomena, and experiences that have kept her and her twin connected. Alice comes to her not only in dreams but also through the appearance of natural phenomena such as birds—very often an eagle—and, particularly, rainbows.

As children they'd spent summers in a cottage in upstate New York situated on a lakeshore where they frequently rode their bicycles. One day they'd just picked bouquets of Queen Anne's lace and were looking up at the sky when they saw a magnificent rainbow shining through the sun. They'd both remembered the experience as something very special, and Alexis described it to me as "a moment of pure joy."

After Alice died, Alexis was driving west one day out of the Sierra Nevada Mountains when she saw "the most intense rainbow I have ever, ever seen" pointing directly toward a small town she'd never been to before. "I immediately knew it was my sister," she said, "telling me which way to go." Subsequently, she bought land in the area, and she has lived there ever since. Now, in dreams, Alice sometimes appears on the hood of a car as the masthead of a ship, still pointing the way—"still," Alexis says, "acting as my guide."

Less than a month after the crash, Alexis was in Mexico, where she bought what she described to me as "a beautiful pair of hand-blown glass angel wings." Although they were very carefully packed, the right one broke on the trip home. Since that time, she says, virtually every time she acquires a pair of anything, half the pair breaks or is lost, and each time that happens she *knows* it's because the spirit of her twin is moving to another realm—as she should, because that's what her spirit is meant to do.

When twins are identical, the physical similarity can also compound the pain and complicate the grieving process. People still sometimes mistake Alexis for her sister, and for a very long time her brother-in-law, who was also on the plane but survived, simply couldn't be with her because, she says, the physical resemblance was much too painful.

That special bond so many twins had described to me was

intensified for Alexis in the aftermath of Alice's death. Feeling their ongoing connection has prompted her to undertake further explorations of her own spirituality. Doing that, and knowing that the deep commitment she and her sister shared in life is still in place, has brought her much peace and comfort.

Summoning Psychic Energy

My openness to the kind of psychic and spiritual powers described by Alexis and other twins was given additional impetus by the supervisor of my graduate clinical training. Tom was a monsignor in the Catholic Church whose cousin was a well-known psychic who'd assisted in many police investigations. As a result, he himself was very much open to, and discussed with me, the extraordinary powers of the mind and how much untapped psychic energy we all have available to us. Subsequently, Tom taught me how to access that power by using hypnosis as a means of tapping into and using our psychic energy for creating constructive behavioral change.

One of the things he said to me was so immediately enlightening that, to this day, I've never forgotten it. "Think," he said, "how powerful the mind is in terms of negative, frightening thoughts that cause mental illness. Then think how powerful the mind can be if you harness that energy for positive use, which is what hypnosis does."

As I'll be discussing further when we talk more about healing, seeing things positively, which is the crux of hypnosis, can have a remarkably powerful effect. By learning to tune into our negative feelings and reframe them in a noncritical, nonjudgmental way, we can open up the channels to our own psychic energy.

We all know what it's like to have a gut feeling, but most of us have been taught to ignore or override those inner feelings.

We think we shouldn't be feeling the way we do. We become judgmental of our own emotions, and we tell ourselves we're just being oversensitive, we're overreacting, we're selfish—or any other number of negative judgments we make about our feelings.

As children, until we're taught otherwise, we're much more likely than we are as adults to accept those gut feelings at face value. When we're hurt, we cry. When we're happy, we laugh. We aren't always second-guessing ourselves or telling ourselves to listen to our head instead of our heart. In effect, we're much more in tune with our own psychic and emotional energies.

The Romantic poets extolled this childish wisdom and understood the spirituality that is expressed by such unmediated emotions and reactions. Or, as William Wordsworth put it in his "Ode: Intimations of Immortality from Recollections of Early Childhood":

> Our birth is but a sleep and a forgetting:
> The Soul that rises with us, our life's Star,
> Hath had elsewhere its setting,
> And cometh from afar.

My dear friend Charlie has two sons, one of whom he has described to me as being an exceptionally spiritual and psychic child whose abilities illustrate the power we all may have available to us when we are open to the possibility of harnessing it. Charlie has told me several striking instances of Gavin's psychic sense. One such story was about the time he went up to his soccer coach after practice and announced, "I think you have a hundred-dollar bill in your pocket." Incredibly, he did. On another occasion they were in a grocery store when Gavin, out of the blue, said to the cashier, "You're from Chicago, aren't you?" And she was.

When she asked how he knew, Gavin simply shrugged and said, "I just knew."

Rather than being disturbed by Gavin's ability, his parents have accepted and encouraged it, and so it has continued to flourish. I believe that all of us are capable of recapturing that primal psychic connection and accessing the kind of knowing that comes from quieting our judgmental mind and trusting our gut feelings. In clinical terms that's what happens in hypnosis, but it's much the same phenomenon as what we experience in meditation, which is one of the primary techniques for opening the mind to greater psychic and spiritual awareness.

The Power to Heal

Several years ago, as an adjunct to my private practice, I began to work with Maria Papapetros, a well-known psychic whose office was in the same building as mine.

I had found that when my patients were so severely afraid of the unknown that they weren't making any progress either in therapy or in life, Maria could help them to see the choices and possibilities that were open to them. This helped to calm them, reduce their fears, and make them more optimistic about their future. Similarly, Maria began referring clients to me, particularly when she felt they were so weighted down and paralyzed by their own problems that they weren't going to be able to act on the information she was giving them.

We recognized that a lot of people are afraid of psychics, of being given answers to the unknown, or simply of the fact that the psychic knows more than they do. Equally, many people are frightened by therapy. They might be unhappy or miserable in a relationship or a job, but they're fearful of doing anything about it. Many simply don't know what to do or how to do it.

We wanted to demystify both therapy and psychic help, so we began holding joint seminars titled "The Mind and the Psyche," focusing on the power of choice and of creating your own reality through the decisions you make. Change is always frightening because you don't know what you're getting into and you naturally wonder whether you might not simply be going from one bad situation to another. Maria helped to ease people's fear and anxiety by letting them know that good things were just around the corner, but they'd have to start walking to get there. When she saw they were afraid either of standing on their own two feet or of defending themselves in an unhappy or abusive relationship, she referred them to me. I then worked with them to help them recognize their own inner strength so that they'd be better equipped to make the changes that would allow them to take better care of themselves both emotionally and physically.

Pam, a patient referred to me by Maria whom I still remember vividly, was trapped in a negative relationship with a totally commitment-phobic man. He kept dangling the carrot of marriage before her and then disappointing her time and time again. I worked with her to have the courage to end it and then suggested that she go back to Maria to see what might be out there for her. Maria exactly described to Pam the man she would meet and marry. Remarkably, she literally met him the next night. Because of Maria's reading, Pam felt she recognized him as someone she should get to know rather than dismiss as simply not her type. As a result, they're married today and have a wonderful daughter. That woman needed to develop the emotional skills that would enable her to leave her unhealthy relationship, but she also gathered confidence and found it comforting to know there was something good on the horizon—or around the corner.

In my work I help people learn to manage their anxieties, calm their fears, and recognize the negative psychic energy they've been carrying as a result of past conflict and trauma. We then work on how they can gain the insight that will free them to use that energy in a more positive and creative way. As a psychic Maria can also show people that they can overcome their negativity and that they do not have to fear making the changes that are open to them. We are both helping people to bypass the skeptical, judgmental conscious mind and open up to the positive psychic energy that resides within each of us.

While the abilities of professional psychics and mediums appear to be naturally more highly developed than those of the rest of us, they, too, tell us that we all have psychic ability. Some of them even point to the fact that we can all connect with the spiritual realm. I believe with absolute certainty that we can not only connect but also make a conscious and deliberate choice to initiate contact and communicate with a departed loved one. In other words, psychic messages flow both ways, and, for that reason, I've chosen to call these contacts "transcommunications."

Later on I'll be teaching you, as I have taught my patients, how to use affirmations and simple meditation techniques to access the psychic energy sources that allow transcommunication to occur. Before you can do that, however, you must want to open yourself up to the possibility that this kind of energy does exist. Like anything you reach for, facilitating transcommunication isn't difficult—if you really want it to happen. The exercises I'll be providing are easy to master. Like putting the key in the ignition of your car and turning it to start the engine, the techniques I suggest will help you to create the vibrational link that allows communication to occur. If you're willing to overcome your fear of the dark (or in this case the unknown) and flip on the light switch, you'll be amazed at the vistas you'll be able to see.

Until you've done that, you'll always be second-guessing yourself. But once you've come to believe it's possible, you'll no longer have any reason to doubt that this kind of psychic and spiritual energy does survive physical death. You'll come to realize that you can continue your relationship with your deceased loved ones by learning how to connect with them. Most importantly, you'll learn how to recognize the messages they send your way.

As you'll discover from the stories I tell, even the most open people, those who have recognized contact and practiced transcommunicaton, can miss the messages that come at them. What I've found to be profoundly gratifying in my work with patients as well as my interactions with friends is when people tell me they would have missed or wouldn't have recognized a sign or message if I hadn't suggested they look for it. My hope is that you, too, will begin to look at things from a new vantage point so that you will be able to see the light of spirit.

Becoming aware of your options can help you to move forward when you seem to be stuck in negative patterns of behavior. In the same way, understanding that you have the option of continuing your relationship with a deceased loved one can have the therapeutic effect of allowing you to deal with your grief in a different way so that you can move on with your life.

Staying in Touch

After my mother died, I began to experience her presence in a variety of ways that are generally known as manifestations. I found that she was connecting with me through energy, animal visitations, music, and dreams.

These phenomena have almost always occurred at a time when I've been thinking of her, on a special occasion, or on a day that brought back the memory of times we'd spent together. Often it seemed as if the thought itself had called up her spirit. Over time, however, I've come to believe that those thoughts at times actually *originate* in the world of spirit. When she was alive, my mother often ended our phone conversations by saying, "I'll be in quick touch." Now I think my thoughts, apparently from out of the blue, are actually coming from the blue beyond—my mother's way of alerting me to the fact that she'll soon be in touch again.

Energy from the Other Side

What was happening in the days, weeks, and months after my mother's death so amazed me that I was compelled to pour myself into the existing literature on afterlife communication. In the course of my reading, I've learned that it's common for these communications to come in the form of a variety of electronic and other mechanical disturbances, which validated the experiences I'd had. For example, one day soon after she died, I was feeling very sad and crying in the bathroom, talking out loud to my mother and telling her how much I missed her, when, without warning, all six of the lights over the vanity blew out at once, two of them actually breaking off in their sockets and shattering so badly that we had to call in a repairman to fix them. Instantly, I felt she had heard me and was reassuring me that she wasn't gone.

On another occasion soon after that, my electric toothbrush stopped working. I kept trying it for four days, hoping that it would somehow miraculously fix itself, but eventually I gave in and bought a new one. When I plugged it in, it refused to go on, but the broken one, which I'd just *unplugged*, went on with no source of electricity at all and started dancing its way across the bathroom counter. I was so shocked that I actually called out to my husband, saying, "You've got to see this to believe it!"

When that happened, I was thrilled because I knew immediately it was my mother keeping in touch. When I was younger, my mother had always emphasized the importance of proper dental care and regular brushing. In fact, she made a point of teaching me a whole tooth-care regime that involved brushing, flossing, and using baking soda. Even during her illness she'd been very concerned about maintaining her self-care and adhering to her long-held grooming habits as much as possible. The one thing she really struggled with was brushing her teeth because it became increasingly difficult for her just to walk to the bathroom to brush. So, when I experienced the inexplicable behavior of my electric toothbrush, I had to laugh because I knew she was coming through. Once more she was emphasizing the importance she placed on brushing your teeth!

I'm certainly as mindful as anyone of the psychological tricks we can play on ourselves that lead us to see a deceased loved one on the street or to hear his or her voice across a crowded room. That kind of wishful thinking is common enough in grief and can be a psychological coping tool. Equally true is the fact that I *wanted* to continue the loving communication my mother and I had always enjoyed. We'd been so much a part of each other's lives, she'd been so steady a support and had shared so many of my hopes, schemes, and dreams, that the thought of her not being there any longer was utterly unimaginable to me. As things began to happen, I of course wondered if they could, indeed, be a product of my imagination. But the sheer volume, however, as well as the repetitive nature and specificity, of the signs I've received since her death has been validation of a connection that goes beyond my own desire. Doreen Virtue, author of *Angel Therapy: Healing Messages for Every Area of Your Life*, has said that "true divine guidance is always repetitive and consistent." I have certainly found that to be true.

These kinds of events have been explained as resulting from the continuance and transformation of energy on the spiritual plane. I'll be discussing that, and other scientific explanations for and explorations of the continuance of life after death, in the following chapter. For now, suffice it to say that I'm not the only one who's been aware of my mother's mischievous method of staying in touch.

My father, the paradigmatic skeptic, has, over time and reluctantly, also been forced to concede that Mom is reaching out to him. One day a few months after her death, he was on his way to visit with Sally, who had been my mother's best friend ever since she and my father had moved to Florida. Suddenly, the automatic lights in his brand-new car stopped working for no apparent reason. As he was driving, he switched them to "manual," but they still wouldn't go on. Then, just as he pulled up in front of Sally's house, they went on of their own accord. The same thing happened several more times over the course of the following year. Each time, he took in the car to be looked at by a mechanic, and each time the mechanic found nothing wrong.

Shortly after the car lights failed for the first time, every radio in his house went on the fritz but began to work again before the repairman had even touched them. When I called him in Florida one day to ask about what had been happening, he said, "I've had everything checked out, and there's nothing wrong with my electricity or the appliances. This is going to sound crazy—and I know

I'm not crazy—but I think your mother's just got to have something to do with what's going on down here. I still can't really believe it, but I can't think of any other explanation for all the really ridiculous things that've been happening lately. For instance, a few days ago I sat down in the den, where your mother and I used to sit and talk. I was listening to the radio, looking at her photographs and thinking about how much I miss her, when all of a sudden the radio stopped working. I checked the outlet, and it worked for the lamp, but not for the radio. Then I realized the radio in the kitchen had also gone off. I replaced the batteries, and it still wouldn't work. The next day, both radios worked like a charm."

I asked Dad what day this had happened, and we were both amazed—although not entirely—to realize that it had been Valentine's Day! Many people report that their mystical connections occur on or around special occasions, and in rooms or places that were significant to the relationship—in this case my parents' favorite room, the den.

Just this past year he was having dinner at Sally's golf club with her, her husband, and their adult son, who was visiting from Boston and had never met my parents. Dad had told Sally about the inexplicable electronic failures he'd been experiencing since my mother died, but Sally, even more skeptical than he, had never taken him seriously and always dismissed his accounts. In fact, when I read her the introduction to this book, she'd said, "That's nice, but do you really believe it?"

At one point in the conversation, Sally's son asked his mother how she had become friendly with Dad. "We met through Helen. She and I were friends," Sally explained. Instantly all the lights in the club dining room dimmed, and then within seconds they brightened again. "You were just talking about Helen," Sally's husband told her. "See," my father said. "I told you. This is what happens all the time." Even Sally the Skeptic was astonished by that demonstration of her friend's spiritual energy. It took four years, but through my mother's persistence Sally finally saw the light.

Over the past four years many people have told me about their own similar experiences, one of the most phenomenal of which happened to a patient of mine when her father passed away. Gabrielle and her dad always had, in her own words, "a very close connection. My mom always said my dad and I were two peas in a pod. So somehow all my life I had to prepare myself for his dying. Throughout my teenage years and even as an adult, I'd have these nights where I'd go to bed and think about how it was going to be when my father died. Somebody was going to tell me father had died, and I would totally freak out. I'd get myself all worked up, and then I'd cry myself to sleep."

When it actually happened, Gabrielle was overseas on business, staying at an old hotel in the English countryside. At one o'clock in the morning, the fire alarm went off, and all the guests were evacuated. The fire department arrived and inspected the building but could find no sign of a fire, so everyone went back to bed. Then, twenty minutes later, at about one thirty, the alarm went off again, and the whole drill was repeated. Soon after everyone had returned to their rooms for the second time, Gabrielle received the call she'd dreaded all her life, telling her that her father had just died. He'd been in a nursing home for some time and was ill but in no apparent danger when she left. His condition however, had deteriorated suddenly. He'd been taken to the hospital and had gone "code blue" in the hospital at eight o'clock New York time and died at eight thirty—just when those alarms had gone off in England. "I didn't realize it for a couple of days," she said, "until I asked what time he'd passed. I felt that he was letting me know he knew where I was and that he was with me. It comforted me tremendously because, even though I couldn't have known he was so close to death, I'd been feeling bad about being away, not being with him at the end." In fact, it's not uncommon for people to experience a dramatic event that they only later discover occurred at the precise time a loved one passed over.

Butterfly Touches

While electrical disturbances are certainly attention-getting, some of the most astounding and heartwarming communications I've had with my mother are in the form of manifestations that I've come to call "butterfly touches." Mom had always loved butterflies—on greeting cards, on clothing, in whatever form she found them. I've always felt that affinity had something to do with her own freedom-loving spirit, and since her death I've come to understand just how powerful and universal a symbol of freedom butterflies really are.

A couple of years ago I saw a stunning dramatization of James Agee's novel *A Death in the Family* on television, and one scene near the end struck so forcefully that I immediately went out to buy a copy of the book. This is the scene, which occurs right after Rufus's father's funeral, in which the little boy's uncle describes something he's seen that struck him as powerfully uplifting.

"There were a lot of clouds," his uncle said, and continued to look straight before him, "but they were blowing fast, so there was a lot of sunshine too. Right when they began to lower your father into the ground, into his grave, a cloud came over and there was a shadow just like iron, and a perfectly magnificent butterfly settled on the—coffin, just rested there, right over the breast, and stayed there, just barely making his wings breathe, like a heart."

Andrew stopped and for the first time looked at Rufus. His eyes were desperate. "He stayed there all the way down, Rufus," he said. "He never stirred, except just to move his wings that way, until it grated against the bottom like a—rowboat. And just when it did the sun came out just dazzling bright and he flew up out of that—hole in the ground, straight up into the sky, so high I couldn't even see him any more. . . . Don't you think that's wonderful, Rufus?"

My own first my butterfly connection occurred on the day my husband, Marc, and I sprinkled my mother's ashes in a canal in Venice, Italy, as she had requested. In fact, that entire day was filled with mystical occurrences. I'd been standing by the canal for a while, waiting for a break in the continuing flow of boat traffic. Just as I determined the moment was right and had started to sprinkle her ashes, the bells in the Church of Santa Maria della Saluta—which means Our Lady of Health—across the canal began to ring. It was an indescribable, electrifying moment.

Then, just at sunset, Marc and I were sitting at a table on our hotel balcony overlooking the spot where we'd sprinkled my mother's ashes when a single white butterfly appeared and flew around our heads, back and forth between us until it had our absolute attention. Then it flew over to the door marked Saluda, or Exit, circled back over our heads, and flew away.

"Wow," Marc said. "*That* was amazing. The only thing missing is a single white dove. Now that would really be a small miracle."

At that very moment I looked across the canal. "Oh, my God!" I exclaimed. "Look, there's a single white bird!"

To our absolute astonishment the bird slowly made its way across the canal, heading directly toward our table. It then flew around our heads, taking the very same path as the butterfly, moved on to the exit sign, and flew away. We were both left speechless. We have never for an instant doubted either at that moment or since, that my mother was acknowledging her passing to us and saying good-bye.

Still later, we were back on the balcony having dinner and watching the full moon rise over the canal. Following its angle, Marc said to me, "I bet the Venetians built that church so that when the moon rises it will center directly over the top." I thought my husband was making an intriguing point, and decided to call the maitre d' over to ask if he were right.

"To my knowledge," the maître d' said, "it only happens once a year, so you're very lucky to be witnessing it. The moon will rise directly over the center of that church with the window with the angel on top and shine right through it onto the canal."

We sat there and watched in awe as the moon continued to rise and then shone through the window, illuminating the very spot on the water where I'd sprinkled my mother's ashes. As the moonlight shone on the canal, it was to us symbolic of her ascent to her next life.

We really felt that we were witnessing a cosmic wonder. For us, it was a purely sacred moment. Altogether, it was a magical day, and it was also the only time I was aware of my mother's appearing as a *white* butterfly. Since then, all the butterfly touches I've experienced have been in the form of a vibrant yellow species with dramatic black markings called the tiger swallowtail. I've since learned that this is just one among approximately twenty thousand known types of butterflies. What confirms my absolute conviction that these butterfly sightings are, indeed, my mother's spirit manifesting itself to me is the fact that her nickname— given to her by her bridge partners in acknowledgment of her fierce competitiveness—was Tiger. Of all the butterfly species, she, incredibly, manifested as the one that was her namesake.

The first live tiger swallowtail I saw appeared in the spring, on my wedding anniversary, while I was sitting on my porch. I later learned that they don't normally appear in our part of the country until the middle of summer. Nevertheless, this one landed on the pink flowers I'd planted in a pot right next to where I was sitting. The minute I saw it I felt an immediate sense of peace, joy, and comfort because my mother had shown up on our special day. Earlier that day I'd also received an unexpected card from a friend with a picture of a large butterfly on it. Then, as we were celebrating our anniversary, Marc and I stopped into our favorite Soho gallery, which we visited only once or twice a year. There on the wall hung a huge painting depicting a woman entirely encircled by butterflies and with butterfly wings protruding from her body.

My mother had always shared in our anniversaries with a call and several cards. This cluster of butterfly manifestations felt like she was sending us, as always, anniversary cards filled with her love and wishes for our happiness, but now she was using a new language. One of my mother's favorite expressions was, "I'm speaking to you in the language of love." Tiger swallowtails now represent to me my mother's new way of sending her love at those times when I need or miss it most.

One of those times was when I was walking back to my office after a visit to the doctor. I'd been dealing with some medical difficulties and was just thinking that this was the first time I'd experienced a major health issue without having my mother there to support me. I was keenly feeling her absence, wishing she could be with me. I started talking to her, saying, "Mom, I can't believe I'm going to be going through this without you. I miss you so much." I was stopped on the corner waiting for the light to change, when a van painted with three enormous tiger swallow-tails pulled up directly in front of me. I have to say that I was truly stunned. I felt my mother had heard me and responded immediately, letting me know that she was there for me.

What really validates these butterfly touches is that they so often occur in direct response to my speaking to or thinking about my mother. One that was truly spectacular occurred on my hus-band's birthday. Because it was a special day, I'd been thinking to myself, "Gee, Mom, when are you going to send us some more of your butterfly magic?" About an hour later I was inside the house when I heard Marc call from out front, "Jane, come quick, you have to see this." I ran down the stairs, and there on our front lawn was a beautiful yellow tiger swallowtail. I really wanted to take a picture of it to have as proof of Mom's spirit contact, so I ran back upstairs to get my camera, hoping the swallowtail would linger long enough for me to snap the shot. When I got back, it was still there. In fact, that butterfly didn't leave for ten full minutes, during which time it allowed me to get close enough to actually touch it while Marc took a picture of me with it. I framed that picture, and to this day I'm amazed each time I look at it because it is evidence of my mother's ingeniously sharing my husband's birthday with us.

My mother, as I've said, was always the guiding force in my life, so these butterfly touches have become symbolic to me of her continuing to carry on as she did when she was alive. She'd always encouraged, supported, amused, and delighted me in a

variety of ways. Now, it's those very same feelings of encouragement, support, amusement, and delight that are evoked every
time one of these butterflies comes into my life. Seeing them
tells me that I can still depend on her to be there when I need
her. Her butterfly touches have mitigated my feeling of being
alone in the world. Just the possibility of seeing a tiger swallowtail
has become exciting to me. Even so, I continue to be confounded
by the fact that they so regularly appear at just those times when
I most need to connect with her—birthdays, anniversaries, and
in times of strife.

Remarkably, I'm not the only one my mother has touched in this
way. During her life, she was always connected to the people
closest to me. Now she continues to get to know them and to
interact with them in her own way. A butterfly, a dream, and an
acute electronic disconnect all combined in a most dramatic fashion when my mother introduced herself to Toni Robino, the
woman who'd been helping me with the early stages of this book.

Toni and I had just spoken on the phone and determined
that we would be working together. Later that day, as she was
sitting on her porch with her husband, a tiger swallowtail butterfly
landed on her right shoulder and stayed there long enough for
her to comment to her husband on the oddness of the experience.
Since I hadn't yet told her of my own butterfly touches, she wasn't
immediately aware of its significance, but she remembered the
incident later, after my mother had alerted her to her presence
in even more startling ways.

She'd asked me to send a picture so that she'd know what
my mother looked like, and during the night following the day it
arrived, she had an extremely vivid dream, which she described
to me this way. "Helen was standing on my back porch, telling

me, 'I'm so glad you and Jane made a connection. You have such similar belief systems; you're going to be good friends.'" When she woke up the next morning, she said, "It seemed so real," and she asked her husband, "Do you think it's possible that Helen is trying to communicate with me?" No sooner were the words out of her mouth than all the electricity in the house went off. "Well, is that enough of an answer for you?" her husband asked.

Suddenly she remembered that her computer was plugged in downstairs in her office, and she was afraid it might have crashed. But the computer was on! There was no logical explanation for this; all the other electricity in the house was off, and when she shut down and unplugged the computer and plugged a lamp into the same outlet, the lamp didn't go on. What had been on the screen at the time of the electrical failure was a file pertaining to my book. "It was really freaky," she said. We both now think that my mother was letting her know, in no uncertain terms, that the kind of communication I wanted to write about was absolutely real.

Sometime after that, Toni was flying to France to teach a workshop. She'd told me she was nervous about doing a good job, and I'd given her some of the same words of encouragement my mother always gave me when I needed them. Toni told me that on the plane she was thinking about what I'd said and wishing she'd had the opportunity to meet my mother. "I took the picture of you and your mother in Venice with me on the trip for moral support," she said. "When I pulled my notebook out of my carry-on bag, the photo fell into my lap. I was sure I'd packed it in an envelope in the zipper compartment, so I was really surprised to see it fall out of my notebook.

"A few seconds later the person behind me started kicking my seat. I turned around to see who it was and ask him or her to please stop. It turned out to be a little blond girl who looked very much like the pictures you'd shown me of you when you were about that age. The really astonishing thing was that she was wearing a T-shirt decorated with a picture of a tiger swallowtail and the word "Venice" stenciled underneath. I couldn't believe it. I knew at that moment that I was not alone and that everything was going to work out. I can't really explain it, but I felt comforted, and most of the anxiety I'd been feeling seemed to melt away. It was as if your mother had been kicking me to get my attention. She certainly has a clear and dramatic way of communicating!"

Although, as I've said, I now realize how universally recognized butterflies are as symbols of freedom, I had not, until recently, met anyone else whose loved one had manifested him- or herself in that way. Just as I was finishing this book, I was browsing in a shop when Paulette, the saleswoman, asked what perfume I was wearing. It was, in fact, called Eau de Butterfly. It was the first new scent I'd worn in years, and I'd been inspired to buy it when I saw a bottle painted with butterflies. I told her about my "butterfly connection" with my mother, and her jaw literally dropped. "That's amazing," she said, "because since my aunt died two years ago, I've seen a butterfly almost every day—either a live one or one in a painting, on a sweater, or on a door. It might be almost anywhere. In fact, there's one butterfly brooch in the shop that keeps changing its position in the display case, even though no one is touching it. When I leave at night, it's facing one way, and when I come back in the morning, it's turned itself around. So far, it's happened three times, and then it just stopped. For a while I couldn't figure out what was going on. Then I realized it must be my aunt Gretchen sending me a sign.

"When I was a little girl, my aunt took me to the house of one of her friends, and it was filled with butterflies. Everywhere I looked there were butterflies—even painted on the toilet. I was so mesmerized that my aunt remembered it. For the rest of her life, she was constantly reminding me of how enthralled I was by those butterflies.

"I always felt she was around, but to me the butterflies were definitely a signal that she was still with me. It just made me feel so wonderful." Clearly, butterflies were very cathected for both Paulette and her aunt.

Here is a final note in this symphony of butterflies. I noticed upon my second or third viewing of the movie *Schindler's List* that in the last scene, when the actors are escorting the actual survivors through the cemetery where victims of the Holocaust are buried, they're surround by a virtual swarm of pure white butterflies. I hadn't actually taken note of that image until I'd had my own butterfly encounters, and I still don't know whether they were a natural phenomenon or one manufactured by movie magic. But I do know that they were there as symbols of the spirit's liberation from the physical body after death.

Loss and Relationships—New Therapeutic Insights

My own experiences with transcommunication have led me to understand that sharing what I've learned with those of my patients who are open to it is simply an extension of the therapeutic work I've done in the past. It has, however, required a shift on my part from a fairly orthodox psychoanalytical frame of reference to a more self-disclosing one. I've started to guide patients who are willing to discover how they, too, can learn to reach out and connect with their loved ones in spirit. My focus, nevertheless, remains the same—helping people heal their relationships, create positive change, and get past their feelings of hurt, anger, disappointment, sadness, and loss. The only difference is that I've broadened the ways in which I—and they—are able to do that.

What I've felt since the death of my mother has also led me to look at loss differently. Through my work with twins, I came to a new understanding and appreciation of the true magnitude and depth of their relationship. From then on, whenever someone told me he or she was a twin, that statement took on a whole new significance with relation to the person's life experience and sense of identity. Virtually the same transformation of understanding occurred as the result of my own experience with loss and afterlife connection.

Clinically, I always understood that the loss of a loved one has a powerful effect on a person's life experience. Loss is not just about the fact that a loved one has died. It's about what happens to you after that—how do you go on when everything in your world has changed? How does the loss change who you were, and how will it change who you ultimately become? Now I have even deeper appreciation for how radically loss can redirect a person's life. When a patient tells me about a loss he or she has suffered, I no longer view it simply as data on family history. Rather, I recognize it as a statement of identity that informs the way that person sees himself and relates to the world.

If your relationship with the one who has died was loving and nurturing, ongoing communication will allow you to continue to feel that love and thus make your grief a bit less painful. If, on the other hand, your relationship was less than ideal, it will give you a further opportunity to come to terms with it and be open to new possibilities.

＊ ＊ ＊

My primary professional goal is to help my patients achieve a more fulfilling life, free of the psychological constraints that might be holding them back. Most of my clinical work, as well as my most recent book, *Gridlock,* has focused on the many ways people get stuck in a bad place or bad patterns. I work at teaching people how they can break through psychological barriers and face their fears in order to feel better.

As children develop and mature, they learn to separate from their parents—particularly their mother—and they gradually become more autonomous and independent. But before they can do that, they have to develop a faith and trust that their mother will still be there when they return. Without that trust they will never have the courage to explore the unknown because they will always be afraid that their anchor, their protector, will disappear.

As adults, the death of a loved one thrusts us into a kind of independence we never asked for and creates a separation that can be both terrifying and overwhelming. As a result many people get stuck in the grieving process and are never able to achieve the resolution that would enable them to carry on with their lives.

One of the gifts of transcommunication that allows us to achieve that resolution is the understanding that our loved one has not disappeared from our life forever. Rather, we still have a way to share his or her love and guidance even after death.

Many years ago, when I was in college, a professor once helped me out by giving me a higher grade than I thought I'd earned because she knew how hard I'd been working. When I asked how I might thank her, she said simply, "You don't have to thank me. Just pass it on." That gift of support touched me deeply. As a healer I've always tried to pass on whatever knowledge I've been fortunate enough to acquire. I believe that knowing our loved ones do not die, but continue to be available to us in spirit, is one of the most valuable and healing gifts I have to pass on.

For me, every loss is about recovery, discovery, and survival—it's a journey through uncharted waters. My hope is that I can help you to navigate those waters more successfully, so that you can arrive at a place where you will feel at peace and able to weather whatever storms you might have to ride out in the future.

2.

From Popular to Profound —Believers, Unbelievers, and the Ongoing Search for Proof

We can never finally know—I just simply believe that some part of the human self or soul is not subject to the laws of space and time.

—CARL GUSTAV JUNG

Since ancient times, some form of belief in, curiosity about, or investigation of the possibility of life after death has characterized humankind. Belief in survival of the soul is a cornerstone of most organized religions. Life after death is the profound hope even of doubters or skeptics, who wish to find a higher meaning than our brief temporal existence can offer.

The ancient Egyptians believed that the *ka,* or life force, accompanied the body throughout its earthly journey and that, at death, it took its place in the kingdom of the dead. To prepare the departed for life in the heavenly realm, the Egyptians placed in the tomb all the necessities of that paradisiacal existence, ranging from furniture to reading material. In ancient Rome specific laws and elaborate customs governing everything from the preparation of the corpse to the mourning rituals of the survivors were intended to ensure that the deceased would have a successful transition to the afterlife. Most ancient peoples, in fact, buried their dead with objects, from bowls to utensils, indicating their belief in an afterworld that closely mirrored existence on earth.

Healers, Helpers, and Demons in Spirit

Primitive cultures from Siberia to Central Asia to North America have looked for both healing and divination to shamans or other priestlike figures capable of allowing their bodies to be inhabited by spirit. Witch doctors, too, are believed to heal the sick by communicating with supernatural agencies responsible for both illness and cure. The voodoo practiced in Haiti and the Santeria of Cuba, the Dominican Republic, and other Latin American countries, as well as the Espiritismo of Puerto Rico, also invoke the healing powers of spiritual possession. The Kabala of the Jewish mystical tradition speaks of impish creatures called golems who, having no will of their own, are bound to do the bidding of those they "inhabit." The Roman Catholic Church has specific rituals for exorcising evil spirits who have taken possession of living souls. And, during the now-infamous Salem witch trials at the end of the seventeenth century, self-styled guardians of morality devised a variety of draconian tests to determine whether or not ordinary men and women were really witches in disguise.

Alexandra, the last empress of Russia, put her faith in the mysterious "holy man" Rasputin to cure her youngest child and only son of hemophilia. Nancy Reagan consulted psychics to determine appropriate courses of action during her husband's term as president. Mary Todd Lincoln held séances in the White House. People from all backgrounds and walks of life faithfully consult those who appear to have the ability to predict the future, communicate with the dead, and in other ways gather information from a realm beyond the bounds of scientific understanding.

The leaders of organized Western religions would prefer that we limit our contact with the spiritual realm to belief in whatever higher power has been designated the organizing principle of its particular denomination or sect, and that our conception of the afterlife be determined by its preferred definition of heaven (or hell). To me, however, it would seem but a short step from believing in a higher power or believing in a heaven or a hell to believing in the survival of consciousness after death or even in our ability to communicate with those in the spiritual realm. If that being and those other worlds exist beyond the boundaries of human perception, is it not possible that other forms of being inhabit those worlds as well? If we can communicate with a higher power through faith and prayer, isn't it possible that we could also communicate with others who reside in the realm beyond our perception? While it's certainly not my intention to question or correct anyone's personal belief system, it does seem to me that the boundaries where one's belief ought to begin or to end can be as amorphous as those early maps that marked the borders of the known world with the warning "beyond this place lie dragons."

Literature and the World of Spirit

The English Romantic poets as well as the American Transcendentalists of the nineteenth century were very much attuned to what they saw as the connection between the individual and the universal, in both a physical and a spiritual sense. William Blake's line from "Auguries of Innocence," "To see the world in a grain of sand," perhaps most vividly and simply describes that profound connection between man and nature, or man and something beyond man.

William Wordsworth, who saw God not as a single divine being but as the presence of the divine in all living things, believed that each of us is born out of that universal soul and that we each bring with us into this life a fragment of divinity. Man's greatest opportunity, he believed, for becoming consciously aware, if only for a fleeting moment, of that divine connection in each of us occurs when we are closest to nature. In nature he saw:

> A presence that disturbs me with the joy
> Of elevated thoughts; a sense sublime
> Of something far more deeply interfused,
> Whose dwelling is the light of setting suns,
> And the round ocean and the living air,
> And the blue sky, and in the mind of man;
> A motion and a spirit, that impels
> All thinking things, all objects of all thought,
> And rolls through all things.
>
> **(From "Lines Composed a Few Miles**
> **Above Tintern Abbey")**

And when we are in nature, it becomes possible that:

> Almost suspended, we are laid asleep
> In body, and become a living soul:
> While with an eye made quiet by the power

47

> Of harmony, and the deep power of joy,
> We see into the life of things.
>
> **(Ibid.)**

In other words, we may be able to become, momentarily, at one with that source of life—the divine—and aware of our connection to it.

Because Wordsworth's beliefs didn't stretch to include survival of consciousness after death, it was in this ability to transcend consciousness during our earthly life that he found our greatest opportunity to become aware of the divinity in each of us. After death we returned, he believed, once more to become one with the universal soul out of which we were born. From then on, as he put it in one of his best-known poems, "A Slumber Did My Spirit Seal," we would be "rolled round in earth's diurnal course / With rocks, and stones, and trees" until such time as we were born again in another form.

In America, the Transcendentalists also espoused this view that the soul of each individual is identical with the soul of the world and contains what the world contains. Perhaps the best-known expression of this thought is contained in Ralph Waldo Emerson's essay "Nature," in which he writes:

> Standing on the bare ground,—my head bathed by the blithe air, and uplifted into infinite space,—all mean egotism vanishes. I become a transparent eye-ball; I am nothing; I see all; the currents of the Universal Being circulate through me; I am part of parcel of God.

While neither the Romantics nor the Transcendentalists were writing specifically about the survival of consciousness or about our ability to communicate with the world of spirit, they were certainly expressing a belief in some form of soul survival and, at least in Wordsworth's case, in a form of reincarnation—whether he called it that or not. Given the affinity of these poets for the natural world as a reflection of the universal spirit, it's also interesting to notice how often those in spirit manifest themselves to us as birds, butterflies, animals, rainbows, and other natural forms.

Popular literature, from the classic to the contemporary, also reflects a universal curiosity about and affinity for all things supernatural. If successful fiction depends upon the reader's willingness to suspend his disbelief in what the author has invented, the continuing success of classic ghost stories, ranging from Wilkie Collins's *The Woman in White* to Henry James's *The Turn of the Screw* to Robert Nathan's *Portrait of Jennie,* certainly attests to the ease with which we are able—even anxious—to believe in interactions with the world of spirit. H. G. Wells's *The Time Machine* and Jack Finney's cult classic, *Time and Again,* are just two examples of time travel fiction, which has succeeded in persuading us to accept man's ability to transcend time and space—a possibility that, as we'll be discussing in a moment, has since been taken from the world of fiction into the realm of scientific exploration. Finally, modern horror stories, perhaps most notably William Peter Blatty's wildly successful novel, *The Exorcist,* speak to our continuing visceral willingness to accept the possibility of demonic possession.

While it's beyond the scope of this book to provide an extensive overview of the role of supernatural phenomena in the history of popular fiction, I do believe it's worth considering the fact that so many revered men of letters and popular writers of fiction have chosen to focus their talents on the possibility that such things exist. Being popular depends upon capturing the interest and imagination of a broad spectrum of the population, and this literature has certainly done that.

TV, Movies, Stars, and Spirits

Perhaps it's because I've been involved with writing this book, but, over the past couple of years, it's been virtually impossible for me *not* to notice how many television programs (in addition to *Touched by an Angel* and *Highway to Heaven,* starring the late Michael Landon, which are predicated on the ability of angels to intercede in the lives of men) have recently featured communications with the world of spirit. *Six Feet Under,* the groundbreaking, Emmy Award–winning HBO series, not only provides viewers with a unique perspective on death but also shows a lead character, Nate, communicating frequently with his dead father. On *Providence* Dr. Sydney Hansen was regularly nagged by her mother from beyond the grave; in the 2001 season finale of *The West Wing,* President Bartlett's deceased assistant returned to give him advice; on *Ally McBeal* the lead character, played by Calista Flockhart, communicated with her dead ex-boyfriend; and on *Once and Again* Lily's late father dropped in from time to time for a chat. What's even more compelling is the fact that *Crossing Over,* the groundbreaking program featuring well-known medium John Edward that originated on the Sci Fi channel, crossed over itself to become a hit on national network television, indicating how widely accepted afterlife communication has become.

Movies, too, have long embraced themes based on angelic visitation, but more recently films like *The Sixth Sense* and *Ghost* have successfully taken a more sophisticated, less romantic, approach to the subject of life after death.

Actress Shirley MacLaine has made no secret of her belief in reincarnation, but she is far from the only well-known figure to be cited as believing in some form of otherworldly communication. Jane Seymour has been quoted in the *Globe* as attributing her being offered the lead part in *Dr. Quinn: Medicine Woman* to the intervention of her late father, who was himself a physician; and Cher is said to have communicated with the late Sonny Bono through the mediumship of James Van Praagh.

Beau Bridges is quoted, again in the *Globe,* as saying, "I believe in the afterlife and I know I'll someday be reunited with my dad [actor Lloyd Bridges] again. . . . He always let us kids know that he believed in God and in an afterlife, too. He's just living in a different place right now."

People magazine has reported that Sandra Bullock, who's had a tough couple of years, also believes that her mother, who died in the spring of 2000, is acting as her guardian angel. Just seven months after her mother's death, the chartered plane on which Bullock was traveling "crashed on landing . . . losing its wings and nose. Bullock walked away without a scratch, for which she credits her late mother: 'I feel like I always have someone watching my back,'" she is quoted as saying.

Dominick Dunne, the well-known popular novelist and reporter of celebrity crime whose daughter was tragically murdered at a time when his own career was on the skids, also recalled for *Biography* magazine that just before she died, he kissed her goodbye and whispered, "Give me your talent." Now, he says, "What

I think she helped me do was *find* my talent. I absolutely believe that. I totally feel she's been my guardian angel."

Again, I could go on citing more and more such stories. Admittedly, I have no way of verifying their truth, but whether they are true or not, we wouldn't be reading these stories if they didn't capture our imagination. To me, it is testimony to the universality of belief in the afterlife connection that celebrities, whom we often look to as role models, and whose behavior is constantly being subjected to public scrutiny, aren't afraid to be forthright about their spiritual connection with departed loved ones. In fact, I've actually come upon an entire book, entitled *X-Rated,* that's devoted to what the subtitle describes as *The Paranormal Experiences of the Movie Star Greats.*

I'm certainly not presuming to suggest that celebrities are more attuned to the spiritual realm than regular folks, but the very fact of their celebrity makes all their experiences—from favorite foods to romantic involvements to afterlife communications—all the more fascinating to the general public than yours or mine might be. Since we tend to idealize, admire, and even identify with such public figures, just reading about their experiences with the world of spirit is, in some way, encouragement for us to reach for our own experiences as well. *If it can happen for them,* we might typically think, *if they can talk to a departed loved one, then why can't it happen for me as well?*

Seekers of Proof

While I was writing this book, a friend who knew about my communications with my mother sent me a magazine article entitled "Messages from Michael,"* which describes the journey from

New Age magazine, November/December 1999.

skepticism to belief of a doctor and his wife whose son committed suicide. Reading it, I was immediately struck by how similar their experiences were to the ones I've had, and by the fact that, like me, the doctor had kept a journal to document the phenomena he could not rationally explain away. If I had required it, his article would have constituted proof for me that afterlife communication is a far more universal experience than most people would believe.

Here are a few excerpts from "Messages from Michael":

[The first Christmas following Michael's death] we took a trip with friends to Morocco . . . and distracted ourselves photographing Moroccan street scenes. We brought along a snapshot of Michael to have with us in our hotel room.

When we had our film developed, the first photograph stopped us cold. It was a blurry picture of Michael! The hair stood up on the back of my neck. Recovering slowly, we realized that it was a picture of the snapshot we had brought with us. . . . But neither of us recalled taking any photos in our room. . . .

I didn't know the significance of this strange event, but I wrote it down. It was soon followed by others. . . .

A book spontaneously fell off the shelf in our apartment. Its title was *Fathers and Sons*. . . .

There were strange electrical disturbances. On two occasions, when [my wife] and I were discussing whether to see a medium, the lights flickered off and on—only in the room we were in.

The dove was my mother's special spiritual symbol, which she had shared with me during her lifetime. I recall making her a wooden dove when I was ten years old, and she cherished this gift. Michael knew about the significance of the dove to me. And now I seemed to encounter doves and dove symbols everywhere.

The eeriest encounter with a dove was at the [golf club]. . . . I was on the fairway when a white dove suddenly appeared next to my ball. I had not seen such a dove anywhere at our country club in my twenty-plus years of playing there, nor had I seen this one alight. I felt chilled as I met the bird's gaze. When I looked away for a moment, it disappeared. I didn't see it fly.

About an hour later, I was on the last fairway. My ball had landed in some bushes, and as I looked for it, I saw the dove again. I was mesmerized by its gaze, and I heard myself asking, "Michael?" My golfing partner called from a distance, and I turned to look. When I looked back, the dove was gone.

After a time, the couple visited mediums who facilitated further communications, providing what was for the bereaved parents ultimate proof that their son was alive in spirit and communicating with them.

At the end of the article, the doctor writes:

We have traveled a long path these past eleven years. It began with a tragic death but led to an understanding that death does not extinguish one's spirit. We know our experiences don't constitute scientific proof of an afterlife. But I hope we can give others some of the comfort and serenity we have found.

Serious truth seekers, believers and skeptics alike, have long since sought to prove or disprove once and for all the possibility of after-death communication.

In 1882 an extremely serious group of such individuals came together to found the British Society for Psychical Research, whose purpose was, according to founding member F. W. H. Myers (writing in *Human Personality and Its Survival of Bodily Death,* his two-volume survey of the first twenty years of the Society's work), to rectify the fact that up to that point

> . . . no adequate attempt had yet been made even to determine whether anything could be learnt as to the unseen world or no; for that if anything were knowable about such a world in such fashion that Science could adopt and maintain that knowledge, it must be discovered by no analysis of tradition, and by no manipulation of metaphysics, but simply by experiment and observation—simply by the application to phenomena within us and around us of precisely the same methods of deliberate, dispassionate exact inquiry which have built up our actual knowledge of the world which we can touch and see.

In addition to Myers, prestigious members of the organization have included the physicists Sir Oliver Lodge, best known for his groundbreaking work in the field of wireless telegraphy, and Sir William Crookes, the discoverer of the element thallium; psychologists such as William James (who in 1884 became a founder of the American Society for Psychical Research), Sigmund Freud, and Carl Jung; Marie Curie; and many other scholars and intellectuals.

The Society was founded at least in part as an answer to the so-called scientific materialism of the previous decade in the hope that its stringent and objective inquiries might prove that not all science necessarily came down in support of materialism. But among its members there were also many skeptics who hoped not to prove, but rather to demolish, any putative evidence of survival after death or of the miraculous in general. Whatever their personal beliefs, however, all these eminent men and women were first and foremost devoted to the spirit of objective investigation conducted in the spirit of scientific inquiry.

Not surprisingly, both the British and American Societies focused on validating or disproving the powers of those who claimed to be "trance mediums" capable of communicating with the spirit world. Among these, Mrs. Leonora Piper is probably the most historically significant as she was the first to show substantial evidence of actually possessing psychic abilities. She lived in Boston and was "discovered" in 1885 by William James, who was on the faculty of Harvard University. Based on James's reports of her apparent legitimacy, Richard Hodgson, a member of the British Society who was considered an expert at exposing frauds, went to Boston in 1887 to continue the investigation. But even Hodgson's most stringent testing failed to disprove her legitimacy, and their well-documented investigations led to James's now-famous statement that "in order to disprove the law that all crows are black, it is enough to find one white crow."

When looking for the kind of proof sought by members of the American and British Societies, one of the surest indications of legitimacy is a medium's ability to deliver information not actually known by the "sitter" or subject that, in retrospect, proves to be true. If the subject is unaware of the information, then the medium, clearly, can't be reading his or her mind—which, skeptics postulate, is one of the ways that clairvoyants are actually receiving their communications. One such medium studied by members of the British Society was Mrs. Gladys Osborne, whose powers were tested over a period of years through various means, among the most striking of which were "proxy sittings," at which the person actually seeking to communicate with someone in spirit was not even present but was represented by a proxy sitter, whose mind could not possibly contain the information the actual sitter was seeking. Mrs. Leonard apparently passed even these rigorous tests with flying colors.

Strict as the Societies' methods may be (and both the British and the American Societies are still very much in operation today), however, these early "experiments" could not be said to carry the weight of scientific proof. Investigations based on scientific knowledge of proved truths about the nature of the universe would have to wait until science caught up with speculation.

Quantum Physics, Astrophysics, Thermodynamics, and the Space-Time Continuum

It should be understood that what is accepted as truth must be based on human perceptions of the moment and remains true only until knowledge has progressed to the point where it becomes no longer true. Or, as Einstein said, "There is no knowledge without experience." It was, for example, a universal truth that the world was flat—until proved otherwise. For thousands of years it went without question that the earth was the center of the universe, until Galileo dared to suggest that it was not and in 1633, was sentenced to life imprisonment for daring to make known his heretical theory that the earth actually revolved around the sun.

We've come a long way since the seventeenth century, both

in our willingness to accept freedom of scientific exploration and in our invention of instruments that allow us to investigate and measure matter and reactions that were inconceivable and unmeasurable less than a century ago.

In the early part of the twentieth century, Thomas Edison was working on a device that he hoped might facilitate communication with those in spirit because, as he said, if life after death did exist, it might be of an electrical nature. In 1920 *Scientific American* published an article providing the details of his device, but it was never built, and Edison died a decade later, leaving further explorations to those who came after.

As modern technology has enabled them to study smaller and smaller particles of matter, scientists are increasingly finding that the rules that apply to the world we see are only approximations of the rules that govern the unseen world of light and subatomic particles.

It's not my intention—and certainly beyond my ability—to explain the complexities of the various discoveries that have allowed even (perhaps especially) the most scientifically inclined among us to speculate that the survival of consciousness is a very real possibility. I can, however, offer you the several scientific truths that have come together to support such speculation.

In 1906, shortly after Einstein announced his theory of relativity, one of his former colleagues, Hermann Minkowski, developed a new paradigm for thinking about space and time. This new paradigm suggested that, because the equations of relativity showed that the coordinates of both space and time had to be considered in order to accurately describe what we see, time had to be considered a fourth dimension—along with length, width, and height. As a result, physicists now routinely consider the world as we know it to be embedded in this four-dimensional space-time continuum, and all events, places, moments in history, and actions are described in terms of their location in both space and time. Space-time does not evolve; it simply exists. When we examine any particular object from the standpoint of its space-time representation, every particle is located along a line that stretches from the past to the future, showing the spatial location of the particle at every instant in time. The line doesn't change with time; it simply exists as a timeless object.

Quantum physics studies the nature of the particles that make up matter and how they interact with one another and with energy. By studying these subatomic particles, scientists have been able to determine that electromagnetic waves, including light waves, behave not only like waves but also like particles, and they have coined the term *photon* to describe the particlelike behavior of those waves. Based upon this discovery, it's been possible to determine that long after stars have died, photons of their energy—or light—continue to exist. And astrophysics has documented the continued existence within our universe of the energy of photons that are more than 12 billion years old.

Add to these discoveries the First Law of Thermodynamics, which states that the sum of kinetic energy, potential energy, and thermal energy in a closed system remains constant—that is, it doesn't run down or die—and it's possible to see how these various theories and discoveries have led to scientific consideration of the possibility that human or psychic energy might continue to exist indefinitely.

If we consider that all matter exists not only in space but also in time, that light or energy more than 12 billion years old continues to exist, and that energy within a closed system remains constant, it is not, I think, unreasonable to suggest that psychic energy also remains constant somewhere within time and space.

Gary E. Schwartz and the Afterlife Experiments

One who has devoted much time and energy over the past few years to contemplating the potential ramifications of just those issues is Gary E. Schwartz, Ph.D., a man with impeccable academic credentials. He holds a doctorate in psychology and psychiatry from Harvard University and has served as professor of psychology and psychiatry at Yale. Most recently he has been a professor of psychology, neurology, psychiatry, and surgery at the University of Arizona and director of its Human Energy Systems Laboratory.

As Dr. Schwartz says in his book, *The Afterlife Experiments,* "In science we hypothesize, we do not believe. And science ultimately does not establish 'proof' so much as provide evidence for or against a hypothesis" (page 10).

Early in 1999 he and his colleagues at the Human Energy Systems Laboratory began the first in what would turn out to be a series of experiments involving five well-known and highly respected mediums, John Edward, Suzane Northrop, George Anderson, Rev. Anne Gehman, and Laurie Campbell. The experiments were conducted under strict laboratory conditions, in order to determine whether or not it would be possible to provide convincing evidence of the survival of consciousness and the possibility of communicating with the dead.

Stringent rules were set up to guarantee that the mediums could not communicate with each other or with their subjects. The mediums could not see their subjects, and, as the experiments continued and the rules became even stricter, their subjects were not allowed to speak for the first several minutes of the readings. In the last phase of the testing, the medium did a meditation and wrote down whatever information was received before even making contact with the subject; the subject was then called on the telephone by the person supervising the experiment (not by the medium), and for the first ten minutes of the reading, the phone was placed on mute so that no sound at all could travel between subject and medium.

All of these precautions and controls were intended to ensure that the medium could not be reading the subject's mind, that there was no way for the medium to deduce reactions through the subject's body language or even through a change in his or her breathing pattern or expression, and that the subject could not in any way be leading the medium through some sort of inadvertent signal.

In his book Dr. Schwartz describes his research and experimentation in fascinating detail. The accuracy of the information the mediums received was often startling, even to the experimenters. In scientific research one of the keys to proving or disproving a theory is that the results of the testing must be predictable and reproducible. Thus, the fact that several of the mediums received significant amounts of the same information may be considered compelling evidence that the results go well beyond the bounds of coincidence. And yet, when asked if he is "advocating survival of consciousness," Dr. Schwartz the scientist replies, "No—what we are advocating is survival of consciousness *research*" (page 268).

Susy Smith's "Great Experiment"

Arguably the mother of all afterlife researchers, Susy Smith was a journalist and the author of thirty books, who spent a good portion of her long life attempting to prove the survival of consciousness after death. When, at the age of eighty-five, she met Gary Schwartz and his colleague, Linda Russek, she had already formulated a plan for leaving a secret message and offering a ten-thousand-dollar reward to the person who was able to correctly receive the information she would communicate from beyond the grave for decoding the message.

Shortly before her death, in 2001, she published *The Afterlife Codes,* her final book, which explains the project and her reasons for engaging in the experiment. The coded message is now housed in the computer of The Susy Smith Project at the University of Arizona, awaiting the successful recipient of her clues from beyond.

And the Search Continues

Social scientists at the turn of the previous century predicted that by the year 2000 belief in the afterlife would have diminished significantly as the result of new scientific discoveries. In fact, just the opposite occurred. By the end of the last century, more people than ever before expressed their belief in some form of life after death.

Science, it seems, has expanded rather than diminished our willingness to believe what once might have been considered unbelievable, and searchers of all kinds are attempting to explore heretofore unexplored possibilities. In recent years, science itself has been giving us both a new vocabulary and a much stronger lens with which to discuss and view the world of spirit. It's as if we've learned a whole new language and at the same time have been fitted with a new pair of glasses that increases our range of vision exponentially.

In the year 2000 an A&E broadcast entitled *Beyond Death* took a look at some of these explorations.

- A thirty-year study at the University of Virginia has produced cases with apparent physical evidence of reincarnation.

- In Atlanta cardiologist Dr. Michael Sabom has documented hundreds of cases that, he says, prove that the soul leaves the body at the time of death. Dr. Sabom believes that near-death experiences are experiences of the dying process, not of the afterlife, and that they occur when the soul is in the process of leaving the physical body.

- At the Valley Medical Center in Seattle, Washington, for more than fifteen years, pediatrician Dr. Melvin Morse has been doing controlled studies of children who are survivors of cardiac arrest. He states that fifteen out of twenty-six children who came to the brink of death had a near-death experience, and he agrees with Dr. Sabom that NDEs are experiences of dying. "When we die," he says, "we suddenly have the ability to communicate with something that most people loosely call God."

- At the Monroe Institute near Charlottesville, Virginia, psychologists and researchers have discovered the possibility of promoting an altered state of consciousness through the use of certain sound frequencies. They've been able to induce states of focused consciousness at a time when the body is sleeping during which the subjects reported having communicated with the dead.

- Andrew Nichols, Ph.D., a parapsychologist and researcher for the Psychical Research Foundation, has been studying ghosts by measuring the electromagnetic levels in the areas of houses where occupants have reported experiencing the presence of a spirit. His purpose is to determine whether the presence of a ghostly being coincides with higher levels of electromagnetic energy.

- At Princeton University, members of the department of engineering have been studying psychokinesis for more than twenty years and have determined that people are apparently able to alter the movements of simple machines, such as metronomes, with the power of their minds, even from very great distances. Robert Jones, Ph.D., director of the Pear Laboratory, where the experiments are being conducted, has said that as a result of these studies he believes that "consciousness can access other parts of space and time than those in which it is physically present."

- Laboratory tests conducted at the University of California at San Francisco Medical School suggest that the seat of consciousness is not the brain. When electrodes were attached to a subject's finger and brain and the finger was pricked, the original impulse to move the finger began in the finger itself and was registered in the brain half a second later. In other words, it was not brain activity that caused the finger to move. But if consciousness does not originate in the brain, then where does it originate?

The search for the seat of consciousness probably lies at the heart of the search to prove or disprove the survival of consciousness after death, for if we can't define consciousness, how can we determine its survival?

With so many searchers devoting so much energy to answering these questions, I can only speculate that science will, at some time in the future, manage to solve the mystery. Until then, however, there is so much anecdotal evidence that, to me, it would seem unnecessarily limiting to shut one's mind to what so many have experienced as true.

I invite you, therefore, if you are a skeptic, to suspend your disbelief long enough to follow me on this journey and perhaps give credence to experiences you might have previously dismissed.

Part Two

Transcommunication
in Action

3.

Seeing Is Believing — Signs from the Spirit Realm

Faith is knowing there is an ocean because you have seen a brook.

—WILLIAM ARTHUR WARD

To set the stage for your own transcommunication, you need to begin by learning to recognize the messages that come your way. Once you have done that, you will be able to start interpreting and translating the special significance of each sign you receive. In essence, you'll be learning to decipher a kind of spiritual Morse code to which only you hold the key.

In the field of psychotherapy we have a clinical term, cathexis, that refers to a person's concentrated investment of psychic energy in a particular concept, idea, image, object, or symbol. That concept, idea, image, object, or symbol is then said to be cathected for that person. You might, for example, be invested in your relationship with another person, whether that relationship is romantic or otherwise. In that case you would be investing an enormous amount of psychic energy in the continuation of that relationship. You might also, however, invest that energy in something as seemingly trivial as the cup of coffee that gets you going each morning. If you really savored that coffee and if you truly believed that you couldn't start your day without it, that java would be truly cathected for you.

I've already discussed the fact that my mother loved butterflies as well as their representation in any form. Butterflies were cathected for her, and by extension they became cathected for me as a representation of my mother. It was therefore, natural that she would come to me in spirit as a tiger swallowtail butterfly, which she knew I would recognize as a sign of her continuing presence.

Only you can be aware of the significance any particular sign or symbol might have held for your loved one, or that your loved one would have known held a special meaning for you. It's up to you, therefore, to be alert to those signs when they appear so that you're able to interpret them and fully enjoy the impact of the connection that's being made. Whatever is cathected for you or your loved one is likely to be his or her clearest channel of communication.

A wonderful, touching, and romantic story that demonstrates this principle at work was told to me by my friend John. He's British, and his first wife was American, but they met—or almost met—in 1959 on the platform of the train station in Munich. It was snowing, and they were both gathering their luggage. They noticed one another but didn't actually speak that day. John is an opera singer, and, four days later, he went to the music library in Munich, where he'd reserved a practice room. Again it was snowing, and as he entered the massive double doors, he saw a young woman with dark hair taking off her black winter coat and shaking out the snow. It was the young woman from the train station, whose name was Amy. This time she approached him, and, assuming he was German, she asked him in German how she could get a practice room. She, too, it turned out, was a singer. After explaining that he was English—and knowing that practice rooms had to be reserved well in advance and were difficult to come by—John invited her to share his.

As John told it to me, they were "destined to meet," and that was, in fact, the beginning of a twenty-seven-year marriage. They both traveled the world performing, and it seemed that virtually every time they met, wherever it was, snow was falling. John still remembers vividly that the day they declared their love for one another, they were walking in the snow.

They were living in New York in 1989 when, tragically, Amy suffered a stroke. John called 911, and he told me that, as they were rushing to the hospital in an ambulance, immense snowflakes were falling. "It was a dark, yellow day, nasty-looking and ominous," he said. "It left me with a feeling of doom, and I knew she wasn't coming back." By the time they reached the hospital, Amy was in a coma, and she died three days later.

She was cremated, and on the day John received a call from the funeral home to pick up her ashes, the sky was bright blue. It was a perfectly clear December day with not a cloud to be seen, but when he left the funeral home with Amy's ashes in a box under his arm, a trail of fine, dry snowflakes fell on the box. Although John is not a man who carries his emotions on his sleeve, he said it was such an anomalous and startling event that he knew it was significant.

Some years later, John remarried on what was again a beautiful, clear winter day. Just as the ceremony ended and people were leaving, it began to snow. He knew then, he said, that Amy was there in spirit, "sharing the day and wishing us well."

While others might have noticed snow falling on these particular occasions, no one but John could have known what a significant role snow had played in his relationship with his wife or have been able to interpret those signs as he did.

As a therapist I'm trained to see similarities and connections and to have insight into psychological patterns and causality that might not be obvious to the layperson. I believe, however, that by becoming alert and paying attention to the signs, large and small, that you might be receiving, you can train your senses to see those potentially meaningful connections between external phenomena that are beyond your control.

Since my mother died, as I've already made clear, she's made her presence known in a myriad of ways—from the dream encounters, butterfly touches, and mechanical disruptions I've already mentioned, to animal manifestations, musical messages, numerical clues, and protective interventions. Each of these manifestations held a special meaning for me because it rekindled some particular aspect of our relationship that allowed me to understand it was still very much alive. Each connection reflects something that we had shared and that, through her sign, we are able to share still.

Being open to the possibility that these kinds of communication could occur and aware of the awesome power psychic energy is capable of producing, I was able to recognize these phenomena rather than dismiss them as nothing more than amusing coincidences. If I'd done that, I believe I would have missed out on a tremendous source of comfort and healing that has profoundly altered the course of my grieving.

Each connection becomes an elixir that alleviates the pain you carry in your heart, subdues the ache of grief, and temporarily puts a smile on your face. My mother's continuing connection has enabled me to adjust to her physical loss—no longer being able to hear her voice, share her laughter, listen to her jokes— because they have created a new kind of psychic and spiritual bond between us.

As a therapist I've worked with many patients who were dealing with loss; I've seen how important it is for them to reach the kind of resolution and closure that will allow them to move forward with their lives. Both personally and professionally, I've come to understand the need we all have to light the few matches we can strike that will illuminate our way to a healthier and happier future.

Learning to Read the Signs They Send

In the preface to his book *After Death Communication,* Louis E. LaGrand, Ph.D., describes the various ways people become aware of communications from deceased loved ones.

ADCs [after-death communications] include sensing the presence of the deceased, feeling a touch, smelling a fragrance, hearing the voice or seeing the deceased, and meeting the loved one in a vision or dream. Messages are also received in symbolic ways, such as finding an object associated with the deceased, unusual appearances or behavior of birds and animals, or other unexplainable happenings which occur at or shortly after the moment of death. Several combinations of the above phenomena may occur within weeks of the death or over a period of years.

In addition, Bill and Judy Guggenheim, in their seminal book *Hello from Heaven,* have categorized and provided anecdotal evidence for the innumerable methods—from visual to olfactory to auditory to symbolic—those in spirit have used to communicate with the living. Those they categorize as symbolic include the appearance of birds, butterflies, rainbows, animals of all kinds, and a variety of inanimate objects such as seashells, coins, and pictures.

While I myself have experienced many of these—and you may certainly experience some that I haven't—I've not actually had a visual encounter with my mother's spirit, although other people have told me about their own remarkable visual experiences. One that stands out was recounted to me at a high school reunion by an old friend who is now a doctor of neurology. Stan told me that within the first week after his father died, he saw him sitting in a rocking chair with a very distinctive expression on his face—one that Stan had never seen in life. He remembers being totally aware at the time that his own eyes were wide open and that he absolutely was not dreaming. He'd never discussed his experience with anyone else in his family until, fifteen years later, his older sister told him about the time when, several years after their father died and after Stan's experience, she'd been staying at a hotel in Los Angeles and their father had appeared to her, sitting in the rocking chair, with an expression that, as his sister described it, was exactly the same as the one Stan had seen.

When I asked him why he hadn't shared his experience with his sister before that, he told me that he'd felt his experience was "very personal" and that it was "very important to keep it to myself. You're almost not sure if it's real," he said, "but it's so real—it's like your own personal religious experience." He said he probably never would have brought it up at all if his sister hadn't told him about her experience. He said that, when he recounted his own vision to her, "it threw shivers through her. It was comforting at the time because she and I have always been very connected. It was a unique experience that validated the very close and at times psychic bond we'd had throughout our lives."

Neither of them has ever shared what they saw with their third sibling. When I asked him why, Stan said, "I didn't know whether it would bother her. I didn't know how it would affect her, and I didn't want to spook her." So, to this day, he and his older sister don't know whether their younger sibling ever had the same experience. But, Stan told me, "things like that" often happened in his family, and he took it very much in stride. In fact, he told me another, equally fascinating story.

It was a Tuesday in the spring of 1997 when he received a phone call from an older cousin, a photographer working for a newspaper, who asked if Stan knew what his father's rank had been in the service during World War II. He did, and he asked why his cousin wanted to know. "Because," he said, "I think I have a picture of him here."

It turned out that Stan's cousin had spent Sunday in the newsroom, where he found a copy of *Newsday* (not the paper he worked for) lying on an empty desk. He picked it up, and, because things were slow, he left early, taking the paper with him. He didn't bother to open it however until Tuesday when, leafing through, he saw a story about World War II and came upon the photo. Initially, Stan said, he was curious but took his cousin's story with a grain of salt, thinking he must be wrong. But his cousin sent him the article, and the photo was, indeed, of Stan's father.

*   *   *

After that, Stan went so far as to call the writer of the article, who told him the only picture accompanying it was of *ships*. "No, Stan assured him," I'm looking at it, and it's a picture of my father." Further research revealed the fact that the photo his cousin had seen appeared in only one edition of the paper, and, to make the story even more amazing, Tuesday—the day he'd finally opened that Sunday paper—was Stan's father's birthday! "It was," Stan told me, "just wonderful, a pleasant reassurance that God exists and that my father was there sending messages directly. To me it meant that he was telling me it was time for him to move on. It didn't feel as if he were leaving me. It was more like he was kicking me out of the nest, telling me he didn't need to watch over me anymore. And that was okay. It was like my own personal rite of passage."

To this day Stan will eagerly document the event with the article and a copy of his father's passport, giving his date of birth and a photograph of him, in order to convince others of the validity of his experience. Not everyone feels the need to offer proof. For some, it's enough to know it themselves. For others, however, myself included, it's helpful, healing, and exciting to show others how real these communications can be.

Tellin' from Helen

My mother used to love sending notes on personal stationery she'd had printed with the heading "Tellin' from Helen." Now the many messages she generates feel to me as if she's continuing to send those loving notes from the spiritual realm.

The range of manifestations I've experienced personally have been so various and so numerous that very early on I decided the only way I'd be sure to remember them all was to record them in a journal, which I've since come to call my "connection catalog." Besides wanting to be sure I wouldn't forget any of them, I also wanted to be sure they weren't simply random occurrences. I would suggest that starting a catalog of your own might be equally useful to you for several reasons.

First of all, recording your experiences can act as a springboard for taking the inexplicable seriously rather than dismissing it as impossible or merely ridiculous. Secondly, my experience— and as you will see, that of others—has been that these events often occur in twos and threes—for example, a dream visit followed by a mechanical failure, or an animal or musical occurrence followed by some other form of symbolic manifestation. Observing these sequences, as well as noting when they occur, can be extremely enlightening.

To illustrate, one particularly memorable series of signs appeared on my mother's birthday two years after her death. On her first birthday after she died, I came down with a bad case of the flu, which, as a therapist, I recognized as a typical grief reaction. It's not unusual for the anniversary of a death or a special occasion such as a birthday to bring up all one's feelings of sadness and loss as if they were brand-new, as if the loss had just occurred. At those times it's rather common for people to become depressed or physically ill. My mother and I had always, without fail, celebrated her birthday together, and so, on that day, I would naturally be missing her terribly. I vowed to do my best to avoid a repeat performance by planning to travel on that date the following year and take her with me in spirit. True to form, she joined in the occasion by providing an extraordinary sequence of connections.

Marc and I checked into our hotel in St. Thomas on her birthday. We often seem to be assigned hotel rooms with either his or my lucky number (which happen to be 3 and 11, respectively), but on this day our room number was 219, *my mother's birthday,* February 19. Later that same day I went to the hotel gift shop to buy a sun hat. I tried on several until I found one that fit me perfectly. When I looked inside to find the price tag, there on the label, in bold letters, was the name of the designer, "HELEN." But that wasn't all. As Marc and I were in our room dressing for dinner, he grabbed a bag of Doritos from the minibar and asked if I'd like one, too. I can't remember the last time I'd allowed myself the dietary indulgence of eating Doritos, but this time I said, "Sure." He tossed me the bag, I opened it, and inside I found a prize like those we associate with Cracker Jacks—a little cardboard butterfly puzzle piece. The next day I purchased seven more bags in the snack bar and opened them all. In each one there was a little gremlin, not a single butterfly.

I did develop a sore throat that year, even in St. Thomas, and it lingered through the week, but it never developed into anything worse than a minor annoyance.

No one contact on that day was of cataclysmic proportions— no parting of the sea, no thunder and lightning from heaven as in a Cecil B. DeMille epic—but taken together they proved to me that I didn't have to experience earth, wind, and fire to feel embraced and loved, and to *know* beyond a doubt that my mother was still very much with me.

In the four years since my mother died, I've filled three books with documentation of the wealth of communications that have taken place between us. Looking back through what I've written has allowed me to see connections between events I mightn't otherwise have noticed. It's also given me a chance to revisit, relive, and reinterpret what I've missed. Once such "missed connection" occurred when I was awakened by a phone call from my father at one o'clock in the morning. He quickly apologized for calling so late and then said, "I had to call because you have to hear this to believe it." With that, he held the phone to his radio so I could hear Louis Armstrong singing "La Vie en Rose," my mother's favorite song, which, as you'll soon see, has been an ongoing leitmotif of our spiritual contact. It seems that Dad hadn't been able to sleep that night and had turned on the radio to his favorite Spanish music station only to hear this song being sung in English by a very American jazz musician. The coincidence was too much even for him to brush off, and he just had to share it with me. I'd entered that visit in my journal under the date May 2, but looking back at my connection catalog in the course of writing this book, I realized that if it was one in the morning, the incident really occurred on May 3, the anniversary of my mother's death!

Many of her most heartening and heartwarming messages do, in fact, occur on special occasions. On my first birthday without her, for example, I was visiting my father in Florida, and we'd gone out shopping for a birthday gift for me. I was looking through a rack of shirts when I discovered a T-shirt decorated with the picture of an angel surrounded by light and holding a magic wand. As I stood there staring at it, I was dumbstruck because the face of that angel was a carbon copy of my mother's face when she was younger. I broke down in tears and showed the shirt to my father, saying, "Who does this look like?" As he answered, "Your mother," he, too, started to cry. We left not only with the shirt but also with gladness in our hearts because we knew my mother had given me a remarkable birthday gift and found a way to spend that special day with us.

I've come to think of her many signs and manifestations as her way of continuing to speak to me in her "language of love." I also realize, however, that had I not been receptive from the start, and had I not documented the many individually small, superficially insignificant, and seemingly coincidental experiences I was having, I might never have understood how significant they really were.

My Mother's Love Song

Simply listing the variety of my own and others' experiences would be enough to more than fill a book, but to help those of you who still might be in doubt to understand why I'm so certain of my mother's continuing presence, I'd like to give a few dramatic examples of one particular manifestation that has been most powerful for me.

My mother's favorite song, as I've already said, was "La Vie en Rose." I loved the song, too, but for some reason I could never seem to remember how it started and was always asking her to sing the first few bars to remind me. One day before she died we were in the car, and I asked her again. She hummed the opening bars, and I suddenly was overwhelmed with profound sadness at the realization of her imminent death and the thought of being left without her. That song, to me, symbolized all the things that I trusted her to know and help me with and that I would no longer be able to turn to her for. It tapped right into my basic fear of not being able to survive without her. In that moment of distress, I said, "Mom, how will I ever remember it without you?" In her ever-supportive style, she replied, "Don't worry, you will."

She's been true to her word. Since her death, I've heard "La Vie en Rose" more frequently than ever before. It seems sometimes as if my life is filled with the beautiful strains of that music. One night, for example, Marc and I had dinner out with my friend Louise and her husband. Louise had brought me a copy of the newspaper from Martha's Vineyard that had printed on its front page Emily Dickinson's poem about butterflies flanked by two butterfly etchings. As we were leaving the restaurant that night, the pianist was playing "Unforgettable," one of my father's favorite songs, and I distinctly remember thinking to myself, *I wish he'd play my mother's song, "La Vie en Rose,"* when, suddenly, he did begin to play it. I was so surprised and taken aback that I stopped and asked him why he'd played that particular song at that particular moment. He answered without hesitation that he hadn't really thought about what he was going to play next, but when he saw me walking toward him, he just knew it had to be that song. I know I don't have the power to will anyone to do my bidding just by thought, but I certainly believe that the power of spirit is stronger than any I might be able to muster.

I also hear her song on special occasions, such as around Valentine's Day, which is just a few days before her birthday. It happened for the first time a couple of years ago when I was in a card shop looking at a Valentine I would have chosen to send her. I was again overcome by grief that she was gone and that I could no longer send her special cards. Sadly, I put the card back on the shelf, at which point the man next to me began to whistle "La Vie en Rose." Just hearing it lifted my spirits and lightened my heart because I knew it was her way of responding to my sorrow and telling me I'd be okay because she was with me.

Most recently, I was having dinner at a New York restaurant with Marc on Valentine's Day, thinking what a perfect evening it had been and that the only thing that might make it even more perfect would be if the harpist played "La Vie en Rose." Five minutes later, she indeed began to play it. Once more I had the heartwarming feeling that my mother was coming through to be with me on this special day. Every time I hear that song, I know my mother is saying, "See, you're just fine, both with and without me."

In addition to his experience with the Spanish-language radio station, my father, too, hears my mother's song on special and significant occasions. One such incident occurred on Father's Day, when "La Vie en Rose" began to play on the radio at the precise moment he picked up his present and began to open it. We both know, whenever we hear it, that my mother is joining us and expressing her continuing love for us.

Many people, when I ask whether they've had a message from a loved one who's passed, have told me, "No, not really," because they don't think the experiences they've had are "enough" to convince them, or because they've dismissed them as nothing more than coincidence. I would urge you, however *not* to dismiss what you've seen, heard, or felt as being only wishful thinking or not significant enough. You will always have a psychological bond, a bond of love, with your departed loved one, but if you discount the possibility of an ongoing psychic and spiritual bond, I believe, you may well be depriving yourself of a truly transforming and healing experience.

The Transformation of a Skeptic

My father isn't the only member of my family who's gone from skepticism to belief since my mother's death. My aunt Ruth also made a complete turnaround once she opened her mind to the possibility that her late husband, Marvin, and her son, Steven, could still connect with her.

When I first started to tell Ruth some of the stories about my contacts with my mother, she was very skeptical, because, she said, "If this can happen, how come I've never received any such contact from either Marvin or Steven?" Just a few days after that conversation, however she called to tell me about an "amazing coincidence" that had just occurred.

"I was going through a stack of old mail and some papers," she said, "and I was thinking to myself, *If Helen's here, why haven't I heard from Marvin and Steven?* Then I picked up the papers, and you won't believe what was on top! It was an acknowledgment to Marvin from a researcher he'd helped with a book more than twenty years ago. I'd never seen it before."

I, of course, told my aunt that the "coincidence" had certainly been a direct sign from Marvin, but she wasn't ready to accept that—until she called again the following week, this time sounding very excited.

"I was telling my housekeeper about the coincidence of finding that acknowledgment to Marvin," she said, "and I told her exactly what I said to you: 'If Helen's here, why haven't I heard from Marvin or Steven?' Suddenly we both heard a crash in the living room. We went to investigate and found that the picture of Marvin and Steven taken at Steven's graduation was lying on the floor. I knew it had to be Marvin and Steven. That photo's been there for years. There's no reason it should suddenly have fallen off the mantle and landed in the middle of the floor."

Remarkably, that was the only photo my aunt had on display of Marvin and Steven together, and it fell off the mantle just a few days before Steven's birthday. It took a crash to convince her, but Aunt Ruth now realizes that her husband and son may have been sending her messages all along and that she'd simply been overlooking them. The fact that the photo that had broken was the only one she had of them together signified to her that they were letting her know they were still together and still connected to her. That realization was amazingly comforting. "You can bet," she told me after reporting the incident, "that I'll pay closer attention from now on!"

When my aunt told me that story, I couldn't help thinking about the photo in my parents' house that had fallen over right after my mother died. And I also remembered an equally significant photographic wake-up call my father had experienced. He'd put some of my mother's ashes into their wedding photo, which was framed behind glass. As he was doing that, he was saying out loud, "Well, Helen, this is the beginning, and this is the end." Sometime during that night the glass cracked straight through my father's image. He was amazed the next morning to see that the glass had split right through him. I said I believed it was the energy of her ashes that had split the glass and that while she had split off from this world, she was still very much with him in the realm of spirit.

Since that time, he's had many other experiences with splitting—his favorite plate, his favorite mug, even his eyeglasses have split down the middle for no discernible reason. In my mother's inimitable way, she gets his attention by splitting his favorite things. I believe it's her way of getting him to miss those things as an extension of his missing her. Despite his sadness at her leaving him, he continues to be amused and heartened by these happenings because he sees them as her way of telling him that her spirit is still with him.

There's Nothing to Fear

In order to hone our receptivity to after-death communication, we have not only to set aside our natural inclination toward skepticism, but also to face our own conscious and unconscious fears. What do we really have to be afraid of, after all? That people will think we're crazy? Maybe a few people will, but with more than 80 percent of the population now stating a belief in some form of life after death,* this is hardly any longer a justifiable accusation.

Or are we simply afraid of looking death square in the face and accepting our own mortality? Very often the death of someone close to us, much less the even-more-unfathomable concept of life after death, marks the first time we're forced to come to terms with the fact that we, too, will die. For many people that's a concept too frightening to deal with. To make matters worse, these people sometimes fear, as did Bill, that any contact with the spirit world might just be a way of preparing them for their own impending death and, therefore, putting them at further risk.

Bill, a patient of mine, had a dream in which a friend in spirit appeared, holding a coffee cup and smoking a cigarette—not in and of itself a particularly frightening image. Bill, however, took the dream to mean that his friend was signaling that his own death was near and was calling Bill over rather than attempting to relate to him in a new way.

On another occasion he was feeling rather low and was meditating before going to bed when he sensed the presence of an older woman, which he described to me as feeling like "an aunt or a godmother," and heard a voice saying, "Oh, he needs a hug." The presence he said, "felt like energy all over my body." He told me that initially it made him feel happy. "It was such a good feeling. But then, at the same time, I was afraid of what was happening. I felt as if I didn't know what I was doing. I must have been putting energy out there and gotten an uninvited re-

*General Social Survey, 1996.

sponse, and I felt I needed to pull back from what I'd tapped into. I was afraid of the contact with the other side."

Bill's response to his experiences made it very clear to me that in order to accept the immortality of the spirit, we first must confront our own mortality. If we don't do that, we're simply burying our heads in the sand and thus burying a part of ourselves with the person we lost, when we could instead be breathing ongoing life into him or her and into ourselves as well.

I say this because, from your very first contact—and even if it proves to be the *only* one—your loved one is letting you know that he or she is alright, and that you'll be alright, too. Knowing that brings with it a profound sense of peace stemming from the understanding that the two of you are still connected in love and in spirit, and that you've ushered in a new phase of your relationship. It is a true rite of passage.

Emme, the well-known author of *True Beauty* and plus-size supermodel, is one whose initial contact with the world of spirit led her to a conclusion diametrically opposed to Bill's. When she was fifteen years old, Emme says, a great-aunt came to her in a dream. Although her aunt was alive at the time, Emme felt that she was acting as a messenger for a family member on the other side. She was in a place that Emme perceived to be heaven. She says that in her heart and soul she knew it was "a beautiful place that people would go to." In the dream her aunt communicated to her that her mother would be going to that place. "My hair was standing up on my head," Emme said. "I was electrified all over my body. I wanted to stay in heaven, but I knew I couldn't."

The very next day, when she got home from a sleepover date at her friend's house, where she'd had the dream, she was told that her mother had cancer. Emme says that she knew immediately her mother would die from her illness. She was shaking and crying, but, because of her dream, she wasn't afraid of the concept of death. "At the time, I hadn't been exposed to the spiritual realm," she said. "Later on, when I'd had some experience with afterlife connections, it all made sense. But even then, it changed the way I was able to handle horrible events. It completely alleviated my flat-out fear of the unknown and deepened my faith in God and my understanding of why we're here." This was a powerful message that has stayed with her throughout her life and enabled her to help others to deal with loss.

Fear only brings negative thoughts and perpetuates our remaining closed-minded in order to relieve our anxiety. It causes us to look upon transcommunication as a sign of our own vulnerability when it would be far more valuable to consider it a sign of our spirit's immortality.

Until we're able to accept the fact that whatever's coming at us is spiritually driven, however, we won't be able to catch and interpret its significance, and its message is likely to drop right in front of us while we're looking the other way, before we've even seen it coming.

A Variety of Signs from the Animal Kingdom

I've already described the many ways my mother has found to continue our communication, including the proliferation of tiger swallowtail butterflies that have entered my life, but her signs from the animal kingdom haven't stopped there. She's also frequently hopped in and out of my life as a rabbit. What's unfolded is that every time I express a wish to see a rabbit, one miraculously appears. My first conjuring occurred one night when Marc and I were driving to the home of our friend Louise, who lived on a back road in a rural part of Martha's Vineyard. It must have been the setting and the season that inspired me, because I said out loud without really thinking, "Gee, I wonder if I'll see a rabbit for Easter." No sooner were the words out of my mouth than a rabbit appeared directly in front of the car, hopped along ahead of us, and turned into Louise's driveway before hopping off. We all laughed because it seemed as if he were escorting us down the road.

Looking back on the incident, I can't even imagine what caused that silly thought to cross my mind, much less to say it out loud. But since then, each time I've wished aloud to see one, a rabbit has appeared—in our front yard, in our backyard, or anywhere at all. I've come to believe that all these bunnies are whimsical manifestations of my mother coming to remind me that she's still very much around. I haven't done a survey of our neighbors to discover whether they, too, are experiencing an unusual influx of rabbits, but I doubt it—especially since I hadn't seen any myself until I began to request their appearance. Unless you're a magician with a hat, it simply isn't possible to make a rabbit appear on the landscape just by wishing it to happen.

For the most part, their purpose is to give me a moment of cheer and delight by confirming my mother's presence in my life. On at least one occasion, however, a rabbit has appeared to validate her awareness of and protective intervention in my father's life. There had been a rash of burglaries in his Florida neighborhood. He's generally an alert and wary kind of guy, so when a woman carrying a baby rang his doorbell one day and told him she'd heard he was looking for someone to clean the house when, in fact, he wasn't, he was quite ready to close the door and send her on her way. But when she asked if she could come in and change her baby—as he later told me on the phone—he couldn't quite bring himself to say no. She went back to her car, theoretically to retrieve the diaper bag, and then she returned with another woman. No sooner were they both inside the house than they literally tackled my father and knocked him down. A scuffle ensued. One woman held him down while the other grabbed what cash and jewelry she could. Then they both ran from the house, leaving him winded, furious, but luckily not seriously hurt.

Later that evening I was walking the dogs and talking on my cell phone, telling my friend what had happened to my father. I was just saying what a miracle it was that he hadn't been badly hurt and that I was sure my mother had been protecting him, when, at that exact moment, a rabbit hopped right across my path. This sort of sequence has now happened so many times that I'm virtually convinced that my mother herself puts the notion of seeing a rabbit into my head and then provides a manifestation to prove its validity. Because of all these sightings, rabbits have come to signify my mother's presence. As a result, I've really come to love them. So imagine my surprise when I recently discovered, while purchasing a necklace with my Chinese horoscope sign, that I was born in the Year of the Rabbit!

I'm certainly not the only one who's experienced these kinds of animal manifestations. Very often, when I tell people about my experiences with the butterflies and rabbits, they have a similar story to relate to me. One of my favorites involved Dr. Dale Atkins, a friend and colleague who had taken in her father's dog, Murphy, after her father became seriously ill with Alzheimer's. One day she mentioned to me that she was going to write a book about her relationship with the dog and how it was her way of staying in touch with her father. After I shared some of my experiences with my mother's spirit manifesting as a butterfly or a rabbit, she became very excited and launched into a story of her own.

It seemed that Dale had been scheduled to appear on a television program to discuss the subject of grief and bereavement, but the program was canceled and she was left with a block of unexpected free time. So, she was sitting by her window, lost in contemplation, when a robin came hopping across the lawn, directly in front of the window. The robin, she said, had been her father's favorite bird. When she saw it, she said, she remembered it was the anniversary of his death. She knew, in that moment, that the robin was her father's way of manifesting himself to her. "I'd just had the thought," she said, "that what I was supposed to be doing with the free time I'd been given was to grieve for him, and as soon as that thought entered my mind, he just appeared. It was his way of letting me know we'd connected. What made the whole experience so incredible was that his favorite song was 'When the Red, Red Robin Comes Bob, Bob, Bobbin' Along.'"

Dale was already receptive to the notion of continued communication with her father. But if she hadn't been, she might never have noticed the robin at all. And even if she did, she mightn't have made the connection. Sometimes communications can be as clear as the nose on your face, but you still won't see what's going on. Once the blinders are removed, however you'll begin to realize what you may have been missing.

Michele, a patient, also told me a particularly touching story about an experience she had in the months just following her mother's death. She was looking out her kitchen window and saw her cat looking in. Next to the cat sat a small bird who simply wasn't moving. Michele couldn't understand why the cat wasn't pouncing on the bird, and she thought the bird must be injured. So she went outside, scooped up the bird, and took it upstairs, where she sat in her mother's rocking chair holding it to her breast. There didn't seem to be anything wrong with it, but it wasn't trying to fly away. Michele then remembered that, both as a child and most recently when her mother was ill, she'd often rested her head on her mother's breast. She was certain that this bird had been sent by her mother to remind her of those tender moments and to let her know she wasn't alone.

Birds have also figured in the life of my friend Charlie, whose son's psychic prowess I described in chapter 1. Since his father died, blue jays, his dad's favorite birds, have invaded Charlie's garden. He was telling me on the phone one day about how annoyed he was by their waking him up with their noise early in the morning, when I said, "Charlie, that's your dad letting you know he's with you."

"You know," he replied, "my dad was a very early riser, and those birds start their music at about six in the morning, which is when he used to get up." From that point on, instead of being irritated by their early-morning chorus, Charlie began to listen for the blue jays, which have come to provide him with a sense of serenity because he understands that they are a sign of his father's continuing presence in his life.

Gabrielle, whose father's death had set off fire alarms in England, recognized a gift from him when she saw it. She had been visiting the cemetery with her fiancé one day close to the anniversary of his death. Just as they were driving out the gate, she noticed a tiny kitten near the gatehouse. "So we stopped to look at it, and it was the cutest thing ever. It just came right up to me and was pawing the ground as if to say, 'Pick me up.' So I picked it up. But I already had two cats in a one-bedroom apartment. I was thinking, *I can't take the kitten; I can't leave the kitten.* Then I just said, 'Fine, I'm going to take the kitten, and I'm going to give it to my mother. She's just going to have to keep the kitten.' So

I took it, and it was just so cute. I kind of think that my dad put the kitten there to give me a reason to go spend time with my mother. My mom has the kitten, and we named her Spooky. When I go to visit, my mother can at times annoy and upset me, but then I sit in my apartment and I think, *I want to see Spooky.* So she's been a good reason for me to visit my mother."

Just a few weeks after Gabrielle found Spooky, when she was house-sitting while her mother was traveling, three more kittens appeared in the yard. They appeared every day until her mother returned, and then they never came back. Now, as her mother's dog is dying, another kitten has appeared, and Gabrielle has told her mother to keep it because, "Daddy gave it to you."

Even my skeptical father has grown to accept the fact that the two herons (a bird name that seems remarkably close to Helen) who've come into his life since my mother's death are more than merely coincidental. One of them appeared on his front lawn, and then; as it crossed the street, it turned its head and stared straight back at him the whole way across. The other appears at least a couple of times a month on the eighteenth hole of his golf course. In fact, herons have become so much a part of his life that he now acknowledges them with the greeting, "Hello, Helen." Because my parents often played golf together, my father believes that she's staying connected by joining him on the golf course. Even though he really needs no further confirmation, the bird often appears in conjunction with some other sign. The episode with his car lights going on the blink, for example, followed just such a heron sighting.

More Varieties of Signs from the Afterlife

While many spiritual manifestations occur as natural phenomena, there is an infinite number of other ways for connection to occur. Carmen Harra, a well-known psychic and the author of *Everyday Karma,* told me about the startlingly unique method her mother found of manifesting herself. This happened just a few months after her mother's death, when the pain of her loss was still very acute. Carmen told me that she'd always been in the habit of buying second-hand cars that invariably gave her trouble, and that, when she was alive, her mother was constantly telling her to just go out and buy the best car. "It's my dream that you buy the best car," her mother had said over and over. So, when she needed a new car not too long after her mother's passing, Carmen decided to fulfill her mother's dream. She drove from her home in Fort Lauderdale to the Mercedes dealership, which was in Miami, only to be told that the model she wanted was on special order and wouldn't be available for six months. She left a hefty deposit and went home, prepared to wait it out. That very night, she sensed her mother laughing and talking to her, saying, "Don't worry, you're going to get that car."

Just a few days later she was in Miami with her daughter for a day of fun and shopping when she received a call on her cell phone from the manager of the Mercedes dealership telling her that he had the car she was waiting for. Someone had apparently placed an order and then changed his mind, so the manager was calling the people on his waiting list, telling them that the person who got there first would get the car. Because she "just happened" to be in Miami that day, Carmen was only ten minutes away. She arrived first and got the car. When she slid in behind the wheel and looked at the sales tag taped to the dashboard, she saw that the name of the person for whom the car had originally been ordered was Alexander. Her mother's name was Alexandra. "I don't need any other proof," Carmen told me. "I felt that my mother was with me and that she had the power to intervene and get me that car, which had always been her dream. I believe that people beyond the physical plane have much more power because they've moved beyond the confines of time and space. If you want to deny it, you will get denial, but if you want to tap into it, you will get power. Skepticism brings only negativity and limitations. If you operate in the land of the spirit, that's one way to access the divinity within you. Belief makes miracles happen."

A patient of mine, Angie, recently described to me a remarkable manifestation that occurred following the death of her brother-in-law Eric. One of eight children, Angie has a large extended family, and shortly before his death her brother-in-law had called upon his siblings and their families to be sure that his two young children wouldn't be deprived of the many experiences he'd hoped to enjoy with them. The family promised that they'd be sure that didn't happen. One of the activities Eric and the kids had always shared was collecting and running an elaborate set of electric trains. True to their promise, the entire family—about twenty-five in all driving a caravan of SUVs—set out the following December for a miniature train exhibit that was being held in Lancaster County, Pennsylvania. The trip itself was an extremely powerful experience for Eric's children. It was a way to keep their father's passion for trains alive and to reinforce the bond they had shared with him. What made the journey even more compelling, however taking it to an entirely different level for the adults, occurred after they had left the exhibit.

Looking for an appropriate evening activity, they saw in the local paper that there was a Christmas village set up in a town some thirty miles away and decided to go. Once more in their SUVs, they were driving over deserted back roads, not really sure where they were going. Suddenly an enormous truck, painted with the logo "ABF," which was the name of the company Eric had worked for, appeared on the road behind, passed their little caravan, and led them over the hills directly to the town they were looking for. As Angie described the experience to me, she said, "It was astonishing. There was not a single other car on the road, and out of nowhere this huge truck appears!" Since that time, ABF trucks have shown up with amazing frequency in the lives of both Angie and her sister.

When she told me about the truck's leading them to their destination, I couldn't help remembering the story I'd been told by Alexis of how her twin sister had led her to her new home. Our loved ones do continue to guide us from the world of spirit. We simply need to be alert enough to read their directions.

While I was writing this book, a professional colleague put me in touch with a woman named Jonna Rae because of the wide variety of communications she'd had with her husband, Paul. Paul died over a period of two years from melanoma. They both knew he was dying and were very open to the world of spirit. "Paul and I spoke frequently about his crossing over," she told me. "I got him watching the John Edward show, and he derived great peace from John's matter-of-fact contact with the deceased. Paul said he'd send me some signs that he was okay." Because of their conversations, Jonna Rae was always aware of the connections he was making and kept a journal of her experiences, many of which she has shared with me.

Even before his passing, Paul and Jonna Rae were aware of a spiritual connection. During his final weeks they drove to a church she thought would be a wonderful place to hold the Celebration of Life Service they had been planning together. His wish, she told me, was to have "a joyful, happy gathering with lots of stories, laughter, and sharing." He loved the church, and on their way home they were discussing the music he wanted to have played. Paul had worked for Disneyland for many years, so "When You Wish upon a Star" was a definite, but he wasn't sure about the final song. She knew he loved the Beatles and suggested "Here Comes the Sun." "It's so beautiful," she told him. "It talks about enduring a very tough time but coming out on the other side to a beautiful sun, and everything's alright. It seems perfect."

"I love that song," he agreed, "but would it be appropriate?"

"Before I could answer," Jonna Rae went on, "we both stopped and stared at the car radio. 'Here Comes the Sun' was suddenly playing on top-forty station. It didn't matter that I hadn't heard it played on the radio in ages. I had to pull the car to the side of the road because I was crying so hard. 'Any questions?' I sobbed. He just shook his head no and squeezed my hand."

Another musical message arrived the very day after he died. Jonna Rae's good friend had flown to San Diego to be with her, and that night they drove out to the beach she and Paul had visited frequently. They were sitting in the car, looking at the stars, and Jonna Rae was crying. The car radio was tuned to a contemporary music station. "I'd just said something like, 'I miss him so much, but I know he's out of pain now,' Jonna Rae told me, when the song 'Spirit in the Sky' suddenly came on the radio. My friend and I stared at the radio, then at each other, and then we started laughing. That song was *so* out of place on that station. Neither of us had heard it in years, but it was so 'Paul' that it was playing for us!"

One of the signs Paul had promised to send her was hummingbirds, because he knew she loved them. "I had shared these signs with a few friends," she said, "and on the day of his Celebration of Life ceremony, several of them were at the church early helping me get everything ready. I had walked to the side of the church to gaze out at a waterfall on the property, and stopped short—there were three hummingbirds darting around the waterfall chirping loudly. That was the *first* sighting. Since then I've seen hummingbirds nearly every day."

Paul, like my mother, also had a great sense of humor, according to Jonna Rae. "For the five days between his death and his funeral, at least three people stayed with me in the house every night. We'd watch the late news together, turn off the TV, and go to bed. And for three mornings in a row, when someone turned the television back on the next day, it had somehow switched itself to the Disney Channel during the night. It's exactly the sort of funny prank Paul, a twenty-seven-year Disneyland veteran, would pull."

One of his most touching messages arrived on the day she was being ordained as a minister in her church. There was one other woman also being ordained that day, and the ceremony took place at a beautiful spot overlooking the ocean and the San Diego cliffs. At one point in the ceremony, Jonna Rae and the other woman, who were sitting on a bench, closed their eyes to pray. When they opened them, Jonna Rae saw on the dark cement bench, not three inches from her leg, a lovely yellow flower. "I turned to the woman next to me," she said, "and asked what kind of flower she'd been given. She said she didn't get one, so I asked the minister who was performing the ceremony why I'd gotten one and she hadn't. 'I didn't give anyone a flower,' he said. We tried to come up with a logical explanation, but there was no wind blowing, and there were no flowers of any kind anywhere nearby. If that flower had been there before I closed my eyes, I certainly would have seen it, particularly since yellow is my favorite color. Paul knew that. He'd loved the fact that I was becoming an ordained minister. I'd been feeling sad that he wasn't there to see it happen. When I saw that flower, cold chills ran up my spine. I felt he was there, and that I was loved and supported."

Paul was certainly there, making sure things worked out for her, when, a year after his death, Jonna Rae was looking for a house to buy. The rent on the house they'd been living in was going up substantially, and she'd decided to use Paul's insurance money to buy something of her own. "The very first home the realtor showed me was *it,*" she said. "Paul had an endearing habit of pasting glow-in-the-dark stars on ceilings—ours, our friends', the ceilings of hotel rooms. In this house, the ceiling of the child's bedroom had been painted deep blue, with nine airbrushed planets in appropriate sizes suspended from it and a smattering of stars peppering the outer reaches of the room's 'galaxy.' I gasped when I saw it. I felt as if Paul had led me to that house and wanted me to have it. I immediately put in an offer and was crestfallen to learn someone else had submitted a bid a few days earlier and it was now in escrow. I looked at a few other houses but never accepted that the 'space house' wouldn't be mine. Then the realtor called—the space house had fallen out of escrow two days before closing. Was I still interested? Within two weeks I'd raced through all the mandatory hoops, and I moved into the house, which I lovingly dubbed La Casita del Sol, two days before Christmas. I knew it was Paul's loving Christmas gift to me, and I feel his gentle presence there constantly."

When Jonna Rae told me these stories, I couldn't believe how many and various her experiences were, and how closely they echoed my own and those of other people I'd spoken to. As she so poignantly said to me, however. "There are no limitations when you love someone. They're always there for you. When someone's in your heart, that door never shuts."

Someone to Watch Over You

I believe that what Jonna Rae said is true, and that one of the ways our loved ones in spirit express their love for us is by making sure that things work out or fall into place. They can do this on important occasions, as Carmen's mother did when she helped Carmen get the car she wanted so badly, and as Jonna Rae's husband, Paul, did by making sure she got the house of her dreams. Sometimes, however, they can also intervene in small, even trivial ways, such as helping us to find a parking space when we need it. On those occasions it would be easy enough simply to think of ourselves as being lucky. I however, have experienced that kind of luck too many times not to realize that it's yet another way my mother has of letting me know she's watching over me.

My first such experience occurred when I was in a taxi on my way to pick up a friend. I wanted to ask her to meet me on the corner so that the cab wouldn't have to wait, but I'd left my cell phone in my office. I was wishing I had a phone so that I could make a couple of calls when I looked on the seat beside me, and there was a phone, obviously left by a previous passenger. A huge smile spread over my face as I picked it up to see if it worked. I made my calls and handed the phone over to the driver to return to its rightful owner.

Another such incident occurred when I'd just had a manicure and had forgotten to take my office keys out of my purse. I was standing in front of my door in a quandary and feeling rather foolish because I knew I'd ruin my manicure if I took out my keys, but I had to let myself in because I was expecting a patient. Just then, our building handyman appeared in the hall, saw me standing there, and asked if he could help me with the door.

Finally, there was the day my father and I were cleaning out my mother's closet. The pile of clothes we'd collected was very heavy, and I said, "Dad, we can't carry all this. We need someone to help us." Just at that moment my father's burly landscaper rang the doorbell and helped us carry everything out to the car.

Since my mother's death I've experienced many of theses strokes of good luck. They've given me the sense that she's somehow still with me, smoothing the rough edges of life or throwing a little spiritual energy my way to help me out when she can.

It's heartwarming to know that she's there acting as my guardian angel. I also know however, that our loved ones can offer us advice and protection on a much deeper and more significant level.

Julie, a patient of mine, discovered just how significant afterlife connection can be when she and her husband received what they now call a life-changing message from their fathers.

Julie is an art director at an international advertising agency who has, for some while, dreamt of devoting all her time to painting. Her husband, Lee, is a marketing executive who has also been frustrated by the limitations of his job. Last summer, they were spending some much-needed vacation time at a beautiful, Japanese-style spa in the foothills of the Sangre de Cristo Mountains. Lee had just come from a marketing meeting in Colorado, and Julie had spent the previous week at an art workshop in Taos, New Mexico. One evening, feeling relaxed and refreshed after a luxurious hour-long soak in the hot tub, they stepped outside to gaze at the sunset.

"It was an extraordinary moment," Julie told me the next time I saw her. "Lee and I had just been talking about how much we wanted to be able to focus on what was most important to us and would give us the most creative satisfaction.

"Then, just as we were looking to the horizon, we noticed a perfectly arced rainbow stretching above the mountains, from one end of the huge blue sky to the other. I was thinking how odd it was to see a rainbow at that moment, since there hadn't been any rain, when, to our amazement, a second, equally magnificent rainbow appeared, curving perfectly just above the first."

Julie's initial reaction was simply to marvel at the beauty and wonder of the natural spectacle. But because she and I had already spent some time talking about transcommunication, she was aware of and open to the possibility of receiving spiritual messages. Nevertheless, it wasn't until later that she made any connection between the unusual appearance of the rainbows and her previous conversation with Lee.

"It suddenly hit me," she said at our next session, "that we'd been sent a message from our fathers, who'd both died in their early sixties, having worked their whole lives at unrewarding jobs without ever having had the opportunity to explore or express themselves creatively. I just knew they were telling us to 'go for that creative pot of gold at the end of the rainbow.' It was a very powerful realization for me, and one I keep coming back to as Lee and I move closer to achieving our dreams."

It's interesting to note that rainbows—along with butterflies—are among the most frequently experienced forms of manifestation. I believe that's because they are so universally recognized as symbols of freedom and hope.

*   *   *

I've certainly felt my mother's protective energy on many occasions. One such intervention that stands out in my memory occurred one day when I drove into the city to tape a thirty-minute television segment. As I was pulling out of the condominium complex where we live, a black raven flew directly in front of my car, and I remember instinctively saying aloud, "Okay, Mom, please keep me safe today." Then, approximately twenty minutes into the half-hour taping, all the lights and cameras in the studio suddenly went down. We had completely lost power, and it took about an hour to get everything up and running again. It wasn't until I got back home and was watching the news that I learned there had been a terrible, multiple-car pileup on the West Side Highway just forty-five minutes before I began my drive home. I realized then that my mother had been protecting me because, without the delay caused by the electrical failure, I might very well have been right in the middle of the accident. I said a heartfelt thank-you to her for watching over me as I'd asked her to do.

On another occasion I was on my way to lead a seminar with a friend. It was the first time I'd be presenting this particular material, and I was so tense that I'd developed a terrible pain in my neck and was barely able to turn my head. At that point I said, "Okay, Mom, I really need your help right now. I'm in such pain." In the next moment the car radio began to play a song by John Tesh called "Mother, I Miss You," which had special significance for me because of the lyric that refers to laughing together, something my mother and I did all the time. Not only was the timing uncanny, but also the song was one I'd never heard on the radio before. I felt such an intense connection with my mother that the pain in my neck instantly disappeared. I felt completely relieved and actually excited about the presentation I would be giving. Like "La Vie en Rose," that song, in that moment, was my mother's way of telling me, "Don't worry; you can, you will."

I know I'm far from the only person to feel this kind of protection. One patient of mine told me a story I'll never forget. His grand-mother had been in Auschwitz during World War II, and he'd grown up believing in many old-world European superstitions, including the belief that wearing a red ribbon or band would ward off evil spirits. The red ribbon was, for European Jews of his grandmother's generation, the equivalent of the evil eye or the Hand of Fatima in other cultures. Not wanting to tempt fate, he put one on his wrist the day his son was born and never removed it until it fell off of its own accord on the morning of his mother's death. He told me afterwards that he knew it had fallen off on that particular day because he would no longer need its protec-tion. The spirit of his mother would be there to protect him from then on.

We've already discussed the fact that children are generally much more open than adults to accepting all kinds of spiritual mani-festations, and I've told you about the psychic abilities of my friend Charlie's son Gavin. Charlie has also told me a powerful story about the remarkable connection between his father and his son. Gavin loves the ocean, Charlie said, and was riding the waves one summer day shortly after his grandfather had passed. When he came out the water, Charlie noticed that he looked a bit shaky and asked him what was wrong. Gavin reported matter-of-factly that a big wave had taken him out and pushed him under the water but that "Grandpa was there, and he pushed me back." Four years later, Gavin still believes his grandpa saved his life. He's repeated the story many times, always exactly the same way, and Charlie says that both his sons believe that they have a "better than ever" guardian angel looking over them and that it's made an important difference for them.

When Charlie told me that story, I immediately thought about reports I'd read of near-death experiences, when people had been told by those in spirit that it wasn't their time and that they needed to "go back." I think that it wasn't Gavin's time that day, and that his grandfather knew it and returned him to the place where he was supposed to be.

One of the clearest, most striking examples of a loved one in spirit sending a protective message was given to me by my friend Sally Kravich, a natural-health expert and the author of *Vibrant Living,* who'd recently bought a house that was in need of much renovation. When Sally told me this story, she prefaced it by explaining that her mother had been a woman with an extremely strong will and enormous energy. Sally said that, at the moment her mother died, all the generators in the hospital went dead for more than three hours. She believed this was a by-product of her mother's intense spiritual energy being released from her body. Sometime later, Sally consulted a friend who practiced psychometry. The man was holding Sally's mother's earring as he said, "Your mom's really got to let you go. It's time for her to get on with her after-death life." With that, the earring literally flew out of the man's hand and across the entire room. Sally's immediate understanding was that no one had ever told her mother what to do, and that she was clearly not ready for her daughter to disconnect from her just yet.

But all that is just to lay the groundwork for the story of an even more amazing experience. Sally's new house, as I said, was in need of much repair, and she'd allocated her somewhat limited funds to taking care of the things that were most important first.

The week after her mother died, the toilet exploded and the pipes burst, sending water cascading from one floor to the next. Those events set off a pattern of necessary repairs, as Sally put it, "on many levels." One morning, as she was lying in bed, the thought came unbidden into her head that she had to repair the Jacuzzi, even though it had not been anywhere near the top of her list of essential repairs. When, within a week, she received a second message from Maria Pappapetros, who is her friend as well as mine, saying that Sally's mother had sent a message telling her to fix the Jacuzzi, she decided not to tempt fate. She had the Jacuzzi fixed and then found out she also had to fix the heater. After that, the gas lines had to be checked. As it turned out, there was a problem with the gas line to the heater, which she also had repaired. Having done that, it was necessary to blow air through the gas lines to be sure they no longer leaked. But when, shortly after the test was completed, Sally walked outside her house, the smell of gas permeated the air. A representative of the gas company was dispatched immediately, and he informed her that *all* the gas lines leaked. The entire house could have blown up at any minute—something she would obviously never have known if she hadn't "thought" to repair the Jacuzzi in the first place.

"My mother," Sally told me afterwards, "was like a lioness in her den. She was going to help her baby come hell or high water." The experience put her more at peace with the loss of her mother because, as she put it. "I don't have to worry. I'm still protected."

Through their many protective interventions our guardian angels can actually help to change the course of our lives by enhancing our ability to make choices for ourselves that we might not otherwise have considered. While each of us is born with infinite possibilities and the gift of absolute free will, some of our life choices are certainly spiritually guided. We are driven to do certain things or to respond in certain ways to particular events in our lives. Whether we think of those choices as resulting from intuition or from the prodding of a guardian angel, I'm convinced that being attuned to the spiritual energy in our lives helps us to make the decisions that will keep us safe. The key is to learn to trust yourself, secure in the knowledge that you're no doubt getting some help.

I believe that our loved ones in spirit really do love us, and that the messages they send us are delivered for a reason. On the most basic level that reason is simply to let us know they're still with us, which helps to mitigate our grief. I also think, however, that they help us in more specific ways. I believe, for example, that my mother was watching over my dad that day he was robbed and could easily have been terribly hurt. I know for certain that when I ask for her help, I receive a response. When I need to feel her presence, she's there for me.

In the chapters that follow I'll be sharing with you the many ways spiritual messages can and do help us heal. They enable us to continue to feel the loving support of those we might otherwise have thought we'd lost. If necessary, they also help us to find closure for the unfinished business that might have been preventing us from moving on with our lives. Transcommunication is not a psychic trick, and it's much more than a "hello from heaven." As I've already indicated, it can actually be a powerful therapeutic tool that's available to every one of us. Because of the unforgettable positive impact such communications have had on my own life and the lives of so many others, I want to help you, too, become more attuned to the spiritual presences in your life.

4.

Conscious Contact —
Putting Out the
Welcome Mat

The guardian angels of life sometimes fly so high as to
be beyond our sight, but they are always looking down
upon us.

—JEAN PAUL RICHTER

Thus far, I've tried to help you become aware of the many startling, astonishing, and subtle ways a loved one in spirit might
make his or her presence known, so that you'll be more likely to
recognize those signs and, as a result, make the connections that
person is trying to generate with you. It's also quite possible however—even quite simple—for *you* to generate those connections
by making a conscious, deliberate choice to request a sign or
communication. That's what we're going to be discussing here.

Conscious contact enables us to open the channels for two-
way communication, such as I've experienced with my mother.
This is the essence of transcommunication—an art you too can
master. With conscious contact you actually become the initiator

rather than the passive recipient of communications from the world of spirit.

It provides you with an opportunity to transform or resume a relationship you may have thought died with your loved one by proactively facilitating the afterlife connection. It isn't difficult; it is not like learning to speak a foreign language. It's more like being the one to start a conversation when you want to speak to someone without waiting for him or her to speak first. It's worked for me and for my patients, and it can work for you, too. I sometimes like to compare what I call "putting out the welcome mat" to learning to ride a bicycle. Once you've found your balance on a bike, you can go anywhere. Initiating conscious contact is like finding your emotional balance. All you need is the willingness to try. If you are willing to reach out, your loved one *will* reach back.

Just recently I was in session with a new patient who had been referred to me for help with her anxieties about upcoming major surgery. I'd given her a healing tape to listen to before the operation and was explaining how helpful it could be.

In the course of our conversation, Denise, who was very much aware of the mind/body connection, said, puzzled, "I don't really understand why I wound up needing this surgery in the first place. I'm a happy person, I don't have a lot of stress, I eat healthy food, and I generally take very good care of myself."

"Well," I said, "have you experienced any kind of loss recently?"

"Actually," Denise replied, "my father died just under two years ago." With that, she went on to talk about what a remarkable man he was, how much she loved him, and how terribly much she missed his presence in her life.

"You know, Denise," I said, "at the beginning of the tape I just gave you, it suggests that you envision all your guardian angels around you offering you their protection. Why don't you ask your father to be there with you? I know if you do, he'll respond." I then went on to tell her about my own afterlife connection with my mother.

When I finished, Denise said quietly, "You're so lucky!"

"That's my point," I replied. "It's not that I'm so lucky. What I'm talking about is something that you can have with your father and that everyone can have available to them as well."

Just Try It

As you know, I did more than just put out the welcome mat when I knew my mother was dying—I actually made her *promise* she'd come visit me. There are two reasons, I believe that our ongoing communication has been so constant. First, our relationship had always been close—we'd been in constant touch and let one another know what was going on in our separate lives. Second, she absolutely knew I was not only open to receiving messages from her in spirit but was actually *counting* on them. So, she makes sure I know and feel her spirit. Thus far she's never let me down when I needed her.

The first time I initiated conscious contact, following my initial plea in the airport, was just a few months after her death. While I was believing all that I'd been experiencing up to that point, I was still hearing a little voice of doubt in my mind. I'd been walking down the street, speaking to my mother, and saying that I really needed to know for sure she was there. About an hour later, I was on the phone with my patient Renee who, I knew, had had many communications from her mother and telling her what I'd done. She said that whenever she asked for assistance, she seemed to receive it. I agreed, saying, "I know what you mean about asking for help." Then, just as she went on to tell me that she always remembers to say, "Thank you, Mom," the phone line went dead, and we were disconnected. In light of my earlier request for certainty, this was a pretty compelling response. It was also a powerful bonding moment for Renee and me, validating our mutual belief that our mothers were ever-present in our lives.

My brother, on the other hand, was, for a long time, unable to embrace the notion that our mother could actually contact us. He simply rejected the possibility of afterlife connection, and so, for a long time, he wrote off the experiences my father and I were having.

Evidently, his lack of communication bothered our mother, who eventually made her feelings quite clear to me in a dream visit by announcing, "I'm angry at your brother. He should call me." The following day, I arrived at my office to find that the light in the little kitchenette had blown out. I knew immediately she was present. Then, as I was standing there, reflecting on the fact that the light's going out had followed one of her dream visits, the glass globe covering the bulb in the hall chandelier fell off for no apparent reason and shattered into a million pieces all over the waiting room floor. At first I was just stunned by all the broken glass. Then I realized that these dramatic manifestations were truly reflections of the intensity of her dream-visit message. I turned to Marc, who is also my professional colleague, and said, "Boy, I guess she's really showing us how angry she is!" While the lightbulb going out in the kitchen had alerted me to her presence, the shattered fixture confirmed absolutely that she was communicating and was punctuating the very message she'd delivered in her dream visit the night before.

I described the whole experience to my brother and explained my belief that it indicated how strongly Mom felt about his not reaching out to her. But it was still another year or two before he was willing to try conscious contact. Finally, one day when I was yet again telling him of a connection we'd made and he was once more saying, "She never talks to me. How come that never happens to me?" I took the opportunity to encourage him once more with feeling, and said, "She's waiting for you to be ready. Ask her for a sign. Just try it. Let her know you're eager to make contact. After all, what do you really have to lose?"

A few days later, he spoke to her out loud. "Hi, Mom," he said. "It's me. I'm asking for a sign. Please let me know you're here." That was it—nothing fancy, no voodoo, no incantations. Just a simple request.

Later that evening he was watching *The Practice* in his living room while another program was taping on the TV in the bedroom. Five minutes before the program was over, just as the segment revealing the ending was to come on, the large picture on the wall behind the sofa where he was sitting came crashing down, knocking the plug from the lamp out of its socket and pitching the room into total darkness. At the same moment the television went off, even though it was plugged into a different socket.

At that point he ran into the kitchen, where the fuse box was located, and discovered that the switch had tripped. He returned it to the "on" position, went back into the living room, and plugged in the lamp. The television went back on. By that time, *The Practice* was over, and he'd missed finding out how it ended.

When I asked him what he thought about this series of events, he said, "It had to be her. There was no reason for the picture to fall off the wall. There was no reason for the TV to go off. And there was no reason for the switch to trip just because the lamp plug came out of the socket." My mother can be quite mischievous, and I like to tease my brother by telling him that, on that occasion, she had to put him in the dark in order to get him to see the light.

The very next evening, he told me, still somewhat confounded by what he'd experienced, he went bowling, and, almost on a whim, he asked for her help. My brother takes his bowling very seriously. He's a member of a league, and he bowls every week, always hoping to make that unmakable spare or to bowl a perfect game. So, his asking her for help with his bowling was his way of continuing the relationship he'd always had with her, which was to ask for her encouragement and support in his various endeavors. His score that night was higher than it had ever been before—beyond his wildest expectations.

As a result of his experiences, he's now much more open to accepting the validity of the connections my father and I describe to him. Some might say he was just having a good night at the bowling alley, but even if he only *believed* she'd heard his request and responded, that psychological bond—his feeling that she was with him—in and of itself was strong enough to help him actualize his ability and perform his best ever.

Once you become less resistant and are willing to consider the possibility that transcommunication is, indeed, possible, the notion that you can "just try it" might be all the impetus you need to put out your own welcome mat, as my brother did. So long as he didn't believe our mother was sending messages, he didn't reach out. Trying it just once was all he needed to do; she was obviously both ready and willing to respond to his invitation.

It might also be possible however that you *are* open to the possibility of communicating with those in spirit but simply haven't thought about doing it yourself. That was the case for a particular patient who consulted with me after the death of her twin sister. The two women were in their thirties at the time, and my patient's sister was married, with a new baby. The loss was unexpected and devastating for her, and it happened shortly after I'd lost my mother. At the time, I hadn't really begun to share my feelings or experiences with my patients, but, for some reason, on this occasion I decided to explore my patient's feelings about life after death. As it happened, she admitted that she was, in fact, open to the possibility, and, following our conversation, she went home and asked her sister for a sign. The light in her bedroom went on and off twice, and, afterwards, she told me not only that she'd felt comforted but also that she'd actually known her sister would come through. Before talking with me, however it wouldn't have occurred to her to ask. Instead, she would have continued to feel a devastating sense of loss without experiencing the relief that connecting with her sister provided.

Put a Candle in the Window

When I talk to patients about the possibility of their staying connected to a departed loved one, I generally ask them first if they've ever been aware of receiving a message, and, if they haven't, I ask if they'd be willing to consider the possibility. If they are, I explain the concept of afterlife connection and talk a bit about my own experience and how it's helped me through my grief. Finally, I suggest that asking for and receiving a sign could have the same kind of therapeutic value for them that it's had for me, and I explain how to go about it.

I suggest that they go out and buy a special candle, one that reminds them of the person they're trying to contact or that has some special significance for them. I suggest that they put the candle in a special place, somewhere they'll see it and that is also connected to their loved one—perhaps a room in the house where he or she enjoyed sitting or spent a lot of time. Then, I tell them to "just ask" by saying something like, "Please, just give me a sign that you're still with me."

Lighting a candle has long been a way of expressing hope and asking for help as well as a sign of invitation. The very expression *a flicker of hope* conjures up the image of candlelight. Candles also play a pivotal role in many religious observations. Roman Catholics light a candle as a way of enhancing the power of prayer when asking for help from God or the Virgin Mary. Jews light candles to commemorate the anniversary of a loved one's death. Psychics, I've been told, believe that the light from a candle helps the energy of the deceased to move on. Lighting a candle not only symbolizes but also creates a sense of serenity, and many people use it as a way to invite a connection with their loved ones in spirit.

My long-term treasured friend and colleague, Dr. Josie Palleja, lost her sister just weeks before the birth of her own child and her niece Lynette's nineteenth birthday. Because her sister and brother-in-law were divorced when Lynette was very young, Josie had always been a coparent to her niece. After her sister's death Josie took over the emotional and financial responsibility for Lynette. Two years later, when she'd graduated from college and was back home living full-time with Josie and her family, Lynette was working at a boring, dead-end job, floundering and not making much of an effort to move out and move on. Josie, for her part, was worn out from caretaking and very angry with her sister who, she felt, had never really taken enough responsibility for her daughter and had on many occasions left Josie to make all the important life decisions for Lynette.

Lighting candles was something familiar to Josie, as it had been a family ritual while she was growing up. Upon the death of her sister, she began a nightly routine of lighting a candle for her. When my mother, whom she'd known all her adult life, passed away, she added a second candle. Then, when her own father died a year later, she began lighting a third. One evening she was virtually at the end of her rope, simply exhausted both mentally and physically, and angrier than she ever remembered being. She went into the kitchen and lit her three candles as she always did, but this time she voiced her feelings aloud to her sister. "Cindy," she said, "I'm really exhausted. I don't want to be angry with you anymore, but you really need to step up to the plate and help Lynette pull it together and get on with her life. You need to help her get a good job, find an apartment, and develop some healthy independence."

The next morning, when Josie went into the kitchen, she saw to her astonishment that the candleholder designated for her sister, which was made out of heavy lead crystal, had cracked completely in half. From the kitchen she walked into the living room, still trying to take in what had happened, and turned on the television. It went on as always, but then the screen went black while the sound continued. Later that morning, while she was driving to work, Josie turned on the radio, which was playing the song she and Lynette had identified as her sister's—a rerecording of "I'll Be Watching You." At that point she just laughed knowingly and said aloud, "Okay, thanks Cindy. I know you heard me."

Later that day Lynette called from work to say she'd been approved for an apartment. The following week she got the job she'd been hoping for. To Josie, that was amazing because nothing had worked out for Lynette since she graduated college. Josie's sister had never taken what Josie considered enough responsibility for her child, and now, within a week of that single plea for help, everything was changing. She told me that afterwards she realized she'd been angry with her sister most of Lynette's life. When she received that sign, however, she felt an overwhelming sense of connection, peace, and comfort because she knew that her sister was finally taking care of her daughter.

That night when Josie lit her candles, she again spoke to her sister. This time she said, "Thank you. I forgive you for all you didn't do. I love you, and you need to keep watching over Lynette." Saying thank you, I believe, is very important. As I tell my patients, if your loved one has acknowledged your need by making himself or herself known, he or she also needs to know that you've understood and acknowledged the message and help.

About four days later a patient who was particularly spiritual and acknowledging of others arrived in Josie's office for her appointment bearing a gift. She'd never brought Josie a gift before, but on this occasion she said, "You've been so helpful, and my husband and I are very appreciative. I've been thinking about you all weekend, and when I saw this, I just felt I had to buy it." The gift was a candle with the Serenity Prayer printed on it. That candle, Josie said, was doubly meaningful because it not only validated for her the sense of serenity and peace she'd finally experienced with her sister, but also she felt, it was providing a replacement for the candleholder that had broken.

While she was telling me about these connections, she suddenly recalled another, earlier occasion when she'd asked for help with Lynette and received it. It seems that while her niece was still in college, she suffered two injuries, both of which required major surgery. On the night before each of the surgeries, Lynette was terribly frightened and was crying. Josie, unable to alleviate her fears, had lit a candle and asked Cynthia to protect her daughter. She didn't just ask that the surgery be successful; she asked that her niece's doctors understand her particular circumstances and take special care of her.

For each of those surgeries, Josie said, the doctors were young physicians—one in his thirties, the other in her forties—who had lost a parent, and who, therefore, had a special empathy for Lynette's distress. The female doctor even held her hand on the way in and out of the operating room. "And what were the odds of that?" Josie asked. She now realized that her sister must have been on the case for each of those surgeries as well.

Sometimes it isn't even necessary to ask for help—we just have to let our loved ones know we miss them, and they'll be there. I've certainly found that to be true, as did Josie the Christmas following her sister's death. It was a time of grief and loss for the entire family but also a time of joy because Josie's daughter had been born just three months before. Josie was shopping for stocking stuffers and decided to buy each member of the family a Beanie Baby. She was standing in front of the display, trying to decide between two possibilities, when she was just overwhelmed by sadness and feeling very much alone. "Oh, Cindy," she said aloud, "I miss you so!" Having said that, she was instantly able to make her choice, and she took home a squirrel named Mr. Nuts to give to her niece. On Christmas morning, when Lynette took Mr. Nuts out of her stocking, she looked at his tag and exclaimed in amazement, "Look, he was born on my mother's birthday." On the tag that hung around the squirrel's neck was printed not only his name but also his "date of birth," January 21. Josie then knew with absolute certainty that her sister had heard her in the store that day and had sent her this sign of her ongoing presence and support.

*　　*　　*

Carmen Harra shared the very moving story of her own candle-lighting experience. Just after her mother died, Carmen said, she was feeling very bereft—thinking, crying, praying, and speaking to her aloud, asking, "Where are you?" and, "Why did you do this to me?" Much the same things that any of us would ask at such a difficult time. She lit a candle and then went into the bathroom, feeling, as she put it, "so in pain." When she returned to the room where she had lit the candle, it had moved, literally, to another table. At that moment, she told me, she felt completely healed. "I knew she was there," she said.

Carmen says that Telekinesis—the impact of energy on matter—is something we all have the power to effect, because the world of energy exists beyond linear time, and in that world we have enormous powers of influence. Personally, I find her assessment of the power of psychic energy not only extremely enlightening but also a validation of all I've experienced firsthand in my own communications with my mother.

Be Sure You're Listening for the Answer

Carmen Harra and Dr. Josie Palleja are both healers who work on a daily basis with people's emotional energy. Because of that, they are extremely connected to their own spiritual energy. Even when we're tuned in, however, the connection isn't always static-free. Not too long ago, for example, Josie was going through a personal struggle and asked her father for a sign that she was making the right choices for herself. The very next day, the air-conditioning in her brand-new car died completely. When Josie told me about the incident, it was because of her frustration with all the things that had gone wrong that day. She just didn't make any connection between having asked her father for a sign and the air-conditioning's failing. I pointed out to her that this was her father answering the request she'd made for a sign the previous evening. "In fact," I said, "it's his way of letting you know that things are heating up before they cool down." Recognizing the sign for what it was not only validated for her the decision she'd made about her life but also alleviated the stress she'd been experiencing that day. The lesson to be learned here, I believe is that even those of us who are most aware of the powers of transcommunication can miss a sign when we're emotionally distracted. All the more reason to write down any incidents that do occur so that we have the opportunity to reconsider—and review—them later.

Tapping into Your Own Psychic and Spiritual Energy

If you are willing to suspend your disbelief long enough to attempt making an afterlife connection, the rewards may astonish you and impact your life in ways you could never have imagined.

That was the case for Michele, the patient we met in the previous chapter whose mother had manifested to her as a bird. Michele was devastated by the loss of her mother, with whom she'd enjoyed a particularly close and connected relationship. Michele's grandmother had lived with her and her mother for twenty-three years, and she'd seen how loving and caring her mother had been during her grandmother's final illness. So, when Michele's mother subsequently became seriously ill herself, Michele took on the responsibility of visiting her every afternoon and making sure that she understood how much she was loved and appreciated.

I knew that when her mother died, Michele would be overwhelmed by feelings of loneliness and emptiness. Because of that understanding I'd already begun to discuss the concept of transcommunication with her. When Michele told me about the bird and her feeling that it had been sent by her mother, I decided to broach the possibility of her initiating conscious contact. I suggested that Michele try asking her mother for a sign. "You were so connected before her passing," I said, "and she's already made her continuing presence known to you, so there's every reason to believe she'll respond if you just ask." We discussed the concept of candle-lighting, and Michele agreed to try it.

When she arrived for her next session, her manner had changed dramatically. "I can't believe this stuff," she exclaimed. "It's *really* fascinating." What had happened is this. Michele, who was staying at her parents' home at the time to be with her father, had lit a candle in the room where her mother usually sat, and said, "Mommy, just give me some kind of sign." Later, she went downstairs to set the alarm clock in the room where she was sleeping. To her utter astonishment, she discovered that the hand of the alarm had moved from 6:00 to 11:00 A.M. "Jane," she burbled, "you know me. I don't get up at eleven o'clock. I'm at work every day by seven fifteen. I knew it was my mother. There was no way that clock hand could have moved by itself."

Michele, with my guidance and support, was able to move from simply recognizing a sign to initiating transcommunication. The experience validated for her that her mother could still feel her and hear her and that she could still hear her mother. Since then, Michele has continued to talk to her, to reach out, and to ask for help in times of strife. By doing that, she's been soothed and comforted in her moments of anguish. Transcommunication is not a cure for grief, but it can serve as an effective analgesic to ease our pain and give us a greater sense of peace.

Michele later told me of another, somewhat amusing, but also heartwarming, experience she had when she again asked for a sign. "Mommy," she said on that occasion, "I know you're here someplace." Five minutes later all the lights in the house went out for absolutely no reason. And again Michele said, "Mommy, if you could just put them back on, that would be great." Sure enough, they went back on. She started to cry, exclaiming, "Oh, my God, Mommy, it *is* you!"

The following year, when Michele's father had also died and she was living in her parents' house, vacillating between whether to renovate it and stay or sell it and move to another state with her then-boyfriend, she heard a bunch of crows making a terrible racket. When she went outside, she saw a red-tailed hawk sitting in the branch of a tree and staring at her. The hawk stayed there for more than an hour, until finally she just greeted it, saying, "Hi, Daddy." As she told me later, "I just knew it was my father."

A few days after that, while she was still uncertain that she'd made the right decision about her future, she went outside and saw the hawk again. Looking up directly at it, she asked, "Daddy, this is the right thing I'm doing, staying here, isn't it?" A moment later, she heard a loud noise. The branch the hawk had been sitting on had crashed to the ground. Michele interpreted that as a validation that she had made the right decision.

When I asked her why she was so sure the sign meant approval of her choice rather than the opposite (a branch crashing to the ground is, after all, a rather negative event), she said, "I just thought he was supporting me." "In other words," I interpreted for her, "it was a validation that you could trust your own gut." And she agreed. Making that connection with her father was therapeutic for Michele because it strengthened her ability to trust her own instincts and reinforced her belief that she was making the right decisions for herself.

Michele loves watching and listening to birds. It's understandable, therefore, that her mother would have manifested in a form so cathected for her. What's even more interesting is that her father did so as well.

Michele knew that her debilitating grief following the death of her mother was making it difficult for her to arrive at certain decisions. Sometimes, however, people don't even recognize why exactly they cannot make the choices or take the actions necessary for improving their lives.

One patient in particular seemed to be both psychologically and literally stuck. Anne Marie had been living with her boyfriend in an abysmal ground-floor apartment they'd both been trying to get out of for years. Their friends had all found better apartments or bought houses in the suburbs while they, despite their best efforts, seemed unable to move on. Instead, they continued to argue about whether they should find another apartment or look for a house, whether they should move farther out of the city or stay closer in. No place was ever right for both of them, and the situation was really beginning to take its toll on their relationship. Now they'd actually found a place they both liked, but the rent was more than they could afford to pay.

During one of our sessions I asked my patient if she'd ever considered asking her father for help. Like many people she hadn't even thought about it but didn't seem entirely closed off to the possibility. Then, to my surprise, she went on tell me that when she was first looking for a place to live and hadn't been certain about taking this apartment, her father was the one who'd encouraged her to do so.

This was something I hadn't been aware of, and Anne Marie had clearly not made the association between her inability to leave that apartment and the fact that, in her mind, her father had endorsed it. I helped her to recognize that by remaining in that apartment she was inadvertently holding onto the only connection she believed she still had with him. Without her realizing it, that apartment had become, for her, the embodiment of her father.

Now, at my suggestion, she lit a candle and asked for his help with her problem. Shortly afterwards, she and her boyfriend were able to negotiate with the landlord to get the apartment they'd wanted for substantially less than the asking price, which meant that they could afford it.

Did her father help Anne Marie get that new apartment, or did the sense of support she got from feeling his presence in her life give her the strength she needed to pursue what she wanted—a better apartment for less than the asking price? While some people might say it was the latter, my belief is that one of the key markers of spirit intervention occurs when things that had previously been fraught with obstacles suddenly work out. I was able to help Anne Marie become conscious of the way her psychological tie to her father had contributed to her remaining stuck in a place where she really didn't want to be. As a result she was able, through conscious contact, to generate an afterlife bond with him that freed her from the bind of living in a place she really didn't want to be.

Some people, however, not unlike my brother, require more persuasion than either Michele or Anne Marie open themselves up to the possibility of asking for help or even asking for a sign. To them, I offer the assurance that you don't *have* to be a believer in order for the process to work, and that, sometimes, receiving the answer you seek will be enough to *make* a believer out of you even if you are a thoroughgoing skeptic.

Such was the case for my patient Karin. Her sister, Ellen, died of a brain tumor as a very young woman. Karin's parents had been divorced when the girls were young, and their mother, who raised them, was, according to Karin's description, extremely self-absorbed and often oblivious to her needs. As a result Ellen, who was five years older than Karin, became her younger sister's lifeline and protector. The two had always been extremely close—bonded in their adversity, so to speak—and so her sister's death had been a hard blow. In fact, it was on the heels of her loss that Karin came to me for treatment because, as she said, her life had virtually stopped in its tracks.

Despite her emotional pain, however Karin remained profoundly skeptical of reconnecting with her sister, even though I'd been urging her to ask Ellen for a sign. Finally she agreed to just try it. She was still doubtful and had absolutely no idea what would happen, but she specifically asked her sister for a sign of her continuing presence. The very next day her sister's son, Karin's nephew, phoned from college to ask for her help with a term paper. She told me afterwards that she'd immediately felt his call was her sister's response to her request, because, although she'd previously reached out to her nephew to let him know she was there for him if he needed her, he had never responded to her overtures. The very act of asking for a sign had been very healing, she said, because for the first time she'd felt she was able to connect with Ellen again.

That initial contact proved to be an icebreaker for Karin, and, about nine months later, she asked for help again. The next time she came to see me, she was bursting with excitement. "Jane," she said, "you're not going to believe this!" She then went on to explain. "I know you keep telling me to ask for a sign, so I finally decided to do it again. The anniversary of Ellen's death was coming up, and I told myself that if I got an offer on my apartment, which, as you know, I've had on the market a long time, that would be a sign. But then I said to myself that I was just being silly, and I sort of put it out of my mind. Well, on the very day of her anniversary, the broker called to tell me he was bringing someone over to look at my place. I waited for them to get there, but I couldn't stay to show the client around because I had to leave for Ellen's memorial service. Just as I was walking out the door, I heard the client say, 'This apartment is just perfect!' I thought maybe I should go back to help cement the deal, and then I thought, *No, if it was meant to be, it will happen.* P.S., She made an offer on the apartment. And what's even more incredible is that the buyer's name is Elena, almost the same name as my sister's!"

When I asked her how the experience had made her feel, she said, "Well, I tell you, I felt as if I'd received a great big hug from my sister. I felt that she was truly with me and that she had heard my request. You know, it's still sort of scary, because I'm such a skeptic, but I got exactly what I asked for."

Asking in Advance

I'm certainly not the only person to have asked in advance that a loved one continue to communicate after he or she has passed over. Fortunately, that isn't a prerequisite for maintaining an afterlife connection. It is, however, a way of letting the person know that his or her contact will be welcome, and of helping to ensure that you yourself will be attuned to receiving it.

As I've already mentioned, I'd been working with Michele prior to her mother's death to help her to prepare for what was to come. I'd suggested that she ask her mother to stay in touch, and we'd discussed the kinds of signs and manifestations she might expect to receive. The day of her mother's death, Michele called to tell me how helpful our conversations had been. That very morning, she said, her telephone had simply stopped ringing. As a result of our previous sessions, she was able to recognize this electronic disconnect as an actual message from her mother, saying that she was on the line and still connected to her. Because of that, what might otherwise have been a negative and demoralizing experience, a sign that nothing in her life was working had been turned into something positive and spiritually healing.

Another patient, Sara, had always had a tumultuous relationship with her father, an alcoholic who could be, by turns, cold and critical, then warm and loving. When he became ill, however she was determined to work through their differences before he died, and she made it a priority to visit him on a regular basis so that she'd have no regrets afterwards.

As his condition worsened and it became clear that he wouldn't live much longer, I took the opportunity during one of our sessions to introduce the concepts of transcommunication and conscious contact, and I shared with Sara my mother's promise to me. As a result, during one of their visits she asked her father with some urgency, "Will you help me when you go to the other side?" "What do you mean?" he asked. "Well," she said, "the way you help me now. The way you look out for me. The way I knew you'd always be there for me, like the way you used to wake me up for breakfast when I was a kid to make sure I got to school on time."

What Sara was looking for was some assurance that her father would continue to be a presence in her life. My being so open, she later explained, was the catalyst that encouraged her to broach the subject. After he died, for two mornings in a row she experienced his shaking her as he'd done when she was a little girl, and she also heard his voice telling her it was time to get up. Feeling that connection, she was able to say out loud, "It's okay, Daddy. I appreciate your help, but I really need my sleep now." Once she released him, he didn't need to awaken her again.

When I asked her how she felt, she told me she'd been jealous because she wanted to go to the other side to be with him and her grandmother. I must have seemed surprised and a bit concerned by that answer, because she immediately went on to assure me that she wasn't wishing to die herself. She was just jealous that he could come this way and go back, and she couldn't do the same in the opposite direction. "But you are," I said. "By using transcommunication, that's exactly what you're doing!" She hadn't seen it that way until I pointed it out, but it was a concept she could accept, and one that was extremely comforting to her.

My friend Linda had also discussed the continuation of some kind of communication with her father on more than one occasion. She told me that he'd been very open to the possibility of life after death but that when he was diagnosed with cancer, he became depressed and the tone of their conversations changed. They had, nevertheless, made a pact that he would stay in touch with her if he could.

On the day she was scheduled to go home to celebrate her parents' fiftieth wedding anniversary, Linda got a call from her sister saying their father had died. She'd been working all weekend on a letter she and her sister had planned to give them as a joint gift detailing all the things about their parents they were grateful for. Now, instead of finishing that letter, she had to begin writing her father's eulogy. It was a devastating experience, she said, and she was crying the entire time, telling herself over and over, "You have to do this." Then she spoke to her father, saying, "Dad, I want to do this for you, but you're going to have to help me."

"For a moment," she told me, "I felt his hands on my shoulders. I felt comforted, as if he were really there."

The next day, when she got up to deliver the words she had written, she was crying so much she couldn't even read what was on the page. She stood on the podium, looked up, and said, "Help me."

Linda described the experience in this way: "An incredible calm came over me. My voice stopped shaking, I stopped crying, and I really got it that Dad wasn't dead. Afterward, everyone who was there, including the priest, told me they couldn't understand how I'd managed to compose myself and share my thoughts and feelings about who he was and what he meant to us all. But I knew it was because Dad had helped me."

Getting Help from Our Guardian Angels

Some of the people whose stories I've told simply asked for a sign of their loved ones' continuing presence, while others actually asked them for help. Asking for a sign is a simple way to invite communication, and sometimes that's all we really need. But sometimes we need more than that; we need some kind of actual help, either in the form of emotional support or something more concrete.

It's just human nature, I believe, that when we're in trouble, or we don't know what to do, or we feel our life is somehow spiraling out of control, we automatically ask for help from a higher power. There are, as the saying goes, no atheists in a foxhole. As I've said, however, I also believe that our loved ones in spirit themselves act as our guardian angels, and that when we ask them for assistance, they will respond.

Callie's Story

Take the case of Callie, an independent, vibrant, and extremely talented young woman whose home life has always been less than ideal. She's the youngest of six children, her next older sibling having died at the age of three-and-a-half just a month before Callie was born. Needless to say, those circumstances created some very mixed feelings in the family surrounding her birth. She's been told that when her youngest living brother, who's five years older than she, first saw her in the bassinet, his only words were, "Where's my brother?" All of her siblings, she says, have always been jealous of her and have treated her as a kind of interloper in the family. Even the family photograph that hung behind the sofa in the living room had been taken before she was born. There was a separate photo of her hanging next to it, as if to symbolize the fact that she was never quite part of the family. Those photos also show that while all the other children look very much alike, she resembles none of them.

Callie's mother was her only and constant supporter, and told her, "You're my special one, my angel from heaven. Without you I wouldn't have survived your brother's death." Callie now thinks that because she was the "healthy replacement baby," she was spoiled by her mother, who was, no doubt, also trying to compensate for the way she was treated by her brothers and sisters. It would be reasonable to assume that her mother's special attention prompted further feelings of rivalry from her siblings, which then caused her mother to treat her even more specially—setting up a classic vicious cycle of cause and effect.

Sadly, Callie's mother was diagnosed with breast cancer when Callie was only thirteen. She lived ten more years and finally died when her daughter was twenty-three. Callie has told me that, a month after her mother's death, a doctor from the hospital phoned her to say that her mother had asked him to call and tell her she was the favorite child.

Sometime later, Callie's father remarried. If she thought her siblings had treated her badly, she now discovered that their jealousy was nothing compared to her stepmother's behavior. On those few occasions when she returned to visit her father at the family home, she was verbally abused, screamed at, slapped, and actually thrown bodily out of the house by this woman. Her father, whom she describes as emotionally immature, not demonstrative, and nonconfrontational, simply ignored what was going on and never attempted to intervene. It's at that point, Callie says, that she truly began to feel like Cinderella.

Possibly because of the tensions at home, Callie turned to alcohol at a very early age, and, after many years of sobriety, she still attends AA meetings. During a rare visit to the family's summer home on Martha's Vineyard, she told her father one evening that she was going to attend a local meeting and might go out for coffee afterward. It was raining that night, and when she got home at about eleven-thirty, her stepmother immediately began to yell at her. "You idiot! Where have you been? You're driving your father crazy, and any man you marry will be driven crazy, too. If we get divorced, it'll be your fault."

Callie ran up to the room where she'd slept many times before and threw herself on her bed sobbing hysterically. The lamp on the dresser had been turned off at the switch on the wall. So, in the dark, she began to pray aloud to her mother. "Mom, help me. I'm so alone. I don't understand what's going on or why I'm so hated. I miss you so much." After about twenty minutes of this, the lamp on the dresser went on, shining on the rain-spattered window in such a way that it formed a cross of light.

"In that moment," Callie said, "I knew it was my mom sending a message that I'd be all right, that I wasn't alone, and that she was watching over me. A sense of warmth and calm washed over me.

"I grabbed a blanket and pillow, turned off the light on the lamp itself, and went into the bedroom directly across the hall, still feeling calm and relaxed, telling my mother, 'I know you're with me. I know I'm not alone,' saying that over and over in my head. After about fifteen minutes, the light in the other room went back on, as if to say, 'You're right. Yes, I am with you.'"

The next morning Callie's father took her down to the beach, put his arm around her, and tried to comfort her, telling her she didn't drive him crazy and not to worry about his getting a divorce. To her, this was "a very special reaching out, the first time he'd done that." Although that didn't change her relationship with her family, from whom she remained essentially estranged, from that point on, she says, she found solace and a new way to cope with them.

Several years later, when she returned to the family home again for Thanksgiving, things went from bad to worse. Her stepmother still resented her and had apparently passed on her bad feelings to Callie's niece, who began to taunt her, saying "What are you doing here?" As she saw how upset Callie was getting, she became even more provocative, saying, "So, are you going to hit me?" Finally, unable to stand the tension any longer, Callie decided to leave. As she approached her father, who was sitting with his back to her in the living room, to tell him she was going home, her niece came up behind her and slapped her across the face. Instinctively, Callie slapped her back. At that point her stepmother came into the room, and Callie just lost it. "I started kicking at her, yelling at her, telling her she was destroying my family, until my brother literally pulled me away and yanked me out of the house. Now everyone in the family believed I was the evil one.

"When I got home, I was terribly depressed, I felt hopeless again, and I really wasn't functioning very well. The next morning was dark and rainy, very much like the night the light went on and off at the Vineyard. Before leaving for work, I got down on my knees and prayed aloud to my mother for help.

"It was garbage pickup day, and when I left my building, there was a huge mound of green plastic garbage bags at the curb. Sitting all by itself, right on top of the mound, in perfect condition, was a Glinda the Good Witch doll from *The Wizard of Oz,* in a pink dress, holding a wand. I was certain it was a sign from my mother that I was going to be all right! So I grabbed that doll before the homeless guy next to me, who was also eyeing it, could get his hands on it. From being in a state of deep depression, I became filled with absolute joy. I walked to work through the rain smiling to myself and showing everyone who'd look what I had found. That day was an absolute turning point in my life, and Glinda is still sitting in my office to remind me that I, too, have a fairy godmother."

When we're at a low ebb, or in severe emotional distress, as Callie was, we need something to let us know that there's hope for a brighter tomorrow, or simply that we're not so alone as we feel at that dark moment. If we're feeling bereft, recapturing the belief that we have not been abandoned in death by the one person who had been our main support in life can be tremendously helpful, as it clearly was for Callie. While the actual circumstances of her life may not have changed, she herself found the strength that allowed her to deflect the slings and arrows cast her way by her dysfunctional family.

To me, it was particularly telling that the sign Callie received came in the form of the good witch from that particular story. That's because I think one of the most compelling messages we can take from *The Wizard of Oz* is that Dorothy had the power she needed all along to take her wherever she wanted to go. Sometimes, however, it takes trials and tribulations to help you recognize and tap into that power. I shared with Callie the notion that her mother was reminding her that she, too, had the power within herself to face whatever troubles came her way. She was also conveying that she would always be there to help and comfort her daughter.

After You Connect, It Gets Easier to Ask

I'm sure we've all been in the position of not having spoken to a friend or a business acquaintance or even a family member for an extended period of time and then finding that we need to ask just that person for assistance or a favor. Calling upon someone with whom you've lost touch to help you can be difficult or embarrassing in life. This is also the case for those who begin to communicate with the dead—even if they're open to the possibility of such communication. But, as we've already seen, it's very often taking that initial plunge that's the most challenging part of the process. Once we have the initial experience, asking for help can become a more and more natural thing to do.

You no doubt remember the heartwarming story told to me by my friend Charlie about how his son, Gavin, had been saved from drowning by his grandfather in spirit. It wasn't too long afterwards that Charlie took a cue from his son and called upon his father himself. Gavin was playing in a T-ball game and putting an enormous amount of pressure on himself to get a home run. He'd already struck out a number of times, and now it was the last inning, and he was once more at bat. Gavin was by that time visibly upset because he was letting everyone down—both himself and his team. As a father, Charlie felt his son's distress and knew he'd be miserable and depressed when the game was over. In what he described to me as a "desperate, pleading moment," Charlie spoke to his father, saying "You've got to make him hit the ball." On the very next pitch Gavin hit the ball out of the park. Charlie said to me, "It was divine intervention. I knew my dad was there beyond a doubt." He described the feeling to me as "overwhelming" and said, "Because it was so powerful, I knew I couldn't waste those favors."

I love hearing Charlie's stories about his sons and their guardian angel, because they so clearly describe the kinds of help we can get from our loved ones in spirit once we've learned to ask. They indicate how powerful a single moment in time can be, whether it's simply bowling a good game or hitting a home run. These moments can then become the catalysts for our ongoing, consistent practice of transcommunication, through which we can literally transform our own lives.

Suzanne did exactly that. She was a new patient who came to see me because of her anxieties, particularly related to fear of flying, and her desire to feel more in control of her life. During one of our early appointments, she began to talk to me about a book I had written. Because I thought it might be helpful, I took that conversation as an opportunity to broach the subject of this book. In the course of our discussion, it emerged that Suzanne had always been open to the power of spiritual and psychic energy and believed in our ability to tap into that power. She then went on to tell me the touching story of the relationship she'd had with her grandmother. Suzanne had gone to her grandmother's house and slept in her room almost every night for the entire last year of her life just so she'd be there if she were needed. Ironically, her grandmother died on one of the very few nights Suzanne was unable to be with her. We talked about that and agreed that her grandmother had planned it that way because she needed the time alone to let go. In fact, Suzanne said, she'd never felt guilty about not being there because she'd always felt it was meant to be. Rather, she was so certain of her grandmother's energy still being with her that she didn't even cry at the funeral or feel dreadfully sad after her passing. But, until I broached the possibility of conscious contact, it had never occurred to her to actually try to reach out and connect with her.

During our next session she told me that our previous talk had helped her to realize she needed to be more in touch with her spiritual self and that she was going to try conscious contact with her grandmother. She went home and did a visualization exercise, much like the one I'll be describing later in this chapter. She pictured her grandmother sitting in a chair with the sun beating down on her, and she asked her to be there for clarity and guidance. As she did that, she said, she "saw" her for the first time. She was smiling, and Suzanne felt the warmth and comfort of her presence in her throat and in her heart. When she wondered aloud to me why she hadn't experienced that presence in her mind, I suggested it was because she'd been feeling her grandmother's presence, not *thinking about* her.

Suzanne said that after that initial experience she felt she'd be able to turn to her grandmother again whenever she needed help. Not long afterward, she told me about an incident that occurred when she and her sister were in yoga class together. Her sister had been complaining about having a really bad stomach-ache, and Suzanne decided to ask her grandmother for help. In her mind's eye she saw her grandmother wink, and, with that, she told her sister not to worry, that she was going to feel better very soon. Sure enough, in about fifteen minutes, her stomach-ache was gone. Suzanne never told her sister why she'd been so sure she'd feel better. "I didn't want her to think that yoga had made me nuts," she laughingly confessed.

Then, at yet another session, she came in and said, "Don't think I'm crazy, but . . . ," and then went on to tell me that she'd asked her grandmother to protect her brother on his pending cross-country flight to visit with her.

With my guidance Suzanne was able to put transcommunication into action in order to reconnect with her grandmother. This afterlife connection helped to alleviate some of her anxieties about herself and her loved ones by demonstrating to her that her grandmother was still able to provide her, and them, with love and protection.

It's always heartening to me when I can help patients like Suzanne, Michele, and Karin become open to their spiritual and psychic energy. By doing this I enabled each of them to incorporate the techniques of transcommunication into their lives. They were then able to enjoy the relief from large and small anxieties such communication can bring. Hearing their stories provides positive reinforcement not only of my own beliefs but also of the fact that sharing them with others is a viable way for me to facilitate their healing.

Feeling Their Presence

In each of the circumstances I've been describing, feeling a sense of connection with a departed loved one is what gave these people the love, hope, comfort, support, reassurance, and relief they required at the time to improve the quality of their lives.

Callie describes feeling a sense of warmth and calm, and of reaching a turning point in her life. Josie felt a heavy burden lifted from her shoulders. Carmen talks about feeling completely healed. Karin felt as if she'd received a "great big hug" from her sister. Anne Marie and Sara found new ways of communicating with their fathers that enabled them to become forces for change and improvement in their lives. In every one of those instances, even when there was some accompanying phenomenon such as a light going off, a candle moving, or something breaking, it was the emotion itself that was the essence of the experience.

To Make Asking Easier

Some of us don't always find it easy to ask, whether it's for a favor, for help, or simply for a sign from a loved one who's no longer living. The people we've met in this chapter have found various ways to make their asking easier—prayer, candle-lighting, or just speaking aloud. But however you choose to do it, whatever "style" makes you comfortable, I urge you strongly to put out the welcome mat and invite your loved ones into your life.

Just because you haven't heard from them doesn't mean they're not there for you. The water doesn't flow into your sink or tub until you turn the tap to release the flow. Asking for a sign can be your way of turning on the tap—or tapping into the flow of psychic and spiritual energy. You don't have to wait until you need something (although I believe your guardian angel will also help you in times of need) just let them know you'd like to hear from them that they're okay.

When you're ready to ask, the following exercise, which I call "Sign Language," will help you to make your connection. It begins with a few minutes of meditation to calm the mind, relax the body, and refresh the spirit.

One of the stumbling blocks we each put in our own path is, as I've said, the fear and anxiety we feel when we contemplate our own mortality. Meditation is one of the tools that can help us to work through those fears and anxieties, to tune out the static of conflicting thoughts and emotions, and, like a pool skimmer, get rid of the toxic garbage, leaving a clear and open channel for connecting with the spirit world. Like hypnosis, it's a technique for grabbing the attention of your conscious mind and keeping it focused on one thought, experience, or scene that's calming and soothing, so that you are able to relax and let go of the conscious ego in order to allow your unconscious the freedom to access whatever spiritual, psychic, or creative energy is unleashed.

Unfortunately, too many people become anxious at the very idea of attempting to meditate. They don't know what to expect, they think it's hard, and they're afraid they'll do it wrong. What you need to understand is that there isn't any right or wrong way to meditate, and that focusing your mind is very much like paper-training a puppy. At first it will keep wandering off, but if you keep bringing it back, your mind, like the puppy, will eventually learn that this is the place to settle down and let go.

1. Close the door, physically and/or metaphorically, on the noise and commotion in your life. Settle yourself comfort-

ably in a place where you won't be disturbed. Assume a comfortable position: seated on a cushion in the traditional cross-legged meditation pose with your hands clasped in your lap or open palmed on your knees, your thumb and forefingers lightly touching, *or* sitting upright in a straight-backed chair, *or* lying flat on your back on the bed or the floor with your arms at your sides and your palms open. Close your eyes and focus on your breath, slowly inhaling and exhaling through your nose.

2. Transport yourself to a place where you feel peaceful and tranquil—a beach, a lake, a boat, a hammock, the mountains—whatever image works for you. Just be sure you avoid picking a place that could conceivably cause you any anxiety. If, for example, you're afraid of heights, don't picture yourself hiking in the mountains or skiing down a slope.

    Let your mind go to that place and keep it focused there, picturing it in as much detail as you can. At this point, many people begin to remember everything they forgot to do that day, and that's when they say, "See, I can't meditate." You need to know that this is happening *because* you *are* meditating and your conscious mind is shaking loose all those worries and concerns that tend to mire you down. Just keep bringing your attention back to the scene in your mind and making it as pleasurable a place as you can conjure up.

    Your meditation can last for as long as forty-five minutes or as few as five—ten to twenty minutes is about average. What matters is the length of time that works for you. Once you're feeling relaxed and comfortable, open your eyes and focus consciously on developing positive expectations about the many ways in which your loved one in spirit might manifest to you.

3. In your mind's eye, picture the person with whom you would like to connect. Make the image as detailed as you can. How is he or she dressed? What is his facial expression? You might even want to hold and look at a photograph to enhance the sense that you're actually addressing him directly.

4. Speak directly to your loved one as you picture him in your mind or look at his photo. Use whatever words make you comfortable:

> I'm ready to connect with you. Please show me a sign.
>
> Please let me know that you're here.
>
> I'm feeling a little sad. Could you send a sign to cheer me up?
>
> I really need you right now; I need to feel your presence.
>
> I know you'll show up, and I'm open to however you'll do it.

The power of the spoken word releases the vibrational energy that facilitates contact.

5. Now clear your mind and wait for a sign. Don't wait with breathless anticipation. Just be in the moment and let go of any specific expectations. Stay tuned-in to any sudden sounds, thoughts, or images that pop up on the movie screen of your mind. When you've received any input at all, no matter how insignificant it might appear to you, document it so that it doesn't slip away.

You may receive the response you're looking for at once, particularly if you're really in need of help or reassurance. But even if you don't, try to stay aware of any unusual feelings or happenings that might occur when you least expect them. Your own response—a sense of wonder, or peace, or warmth, or amazement— will be your best guide to knowing your loved one is there.

Once you've made your initial contact, having asked for and received a sign, it might be useful to include another exercise, which has been referred to by numerous psychics as "harnessing the protective power of the white light." When you're opening a channel for the energy of spirit to come through, it's important that you protect yourself from the negative energy of souls that haven't completely passed over, which can create interference with your afterlife connection. This exercise takes no more that thirty to ninety seconds to complete; and I think of it is the equivalent of cleaning a VCR tape to ensure that a clear picture comes through.

1. Settle yourself comfortably in a seated position, on the floor or in a chair, and close your eyes.
2. Visualize a stream of white light stretching down to you from the sky above and enveloping you from the top of your head to the bottom of your feet, as if you were taking a shower in the light. Imagine it moving down and around each limb, across your front and back, so that your entire body is insulated and protected.
3. Complete the exercise by saying to yourself, "I am completely safe and protected in the white light."

Ask, and They Will Provide

For some people, making a single contact can be enough to release them from doubt, anxiety, or pain. Others might need to ask again and again. For still others, making the initial overture might be enough to keep their loved one returning without being asked again. It's been my experience that whatever your needs or desires, they will be recognized and met. Facilitating conscious contact and connecting with your loved ones through the signs they send can enhance and enrich your life, bring you a sense of peace, and help you to move beyond your grief.

My patient Angie, who lost her brother-in-law Eric and found herself and her family led through the hills of Pennsylvania by a truck from Eric's company, ABF, continues to receive signs whenever she needs or asks for them. Just recently, on Eric's birthday, she was driving in her car when she realized that she hadn't gotten a message from him that day and thought it was unusual. She spoke to him aloud, saying, "How come we haven't heard from you today? Please, just let me know that you're here." No sooner had the words passed her lips than a car pulled up next to hers bearing the license plate "ABF 2002." That unmistakable connection reassured her that she could actually rely on Eric's continuing presence at those times when she looked to him to be there.

5.

Dream Visits — Meetings in the Spirit World

I'll see you in my dreams—

—GUS KAHN

Once you've put out the welcome mat and initiated conscious contact with your loved one, you can invite—or you might find that you're already receiving—dream visits from the world of spirit. The first step to enjoying this kind of transcommunication is, as with recognizing any kind of sign, coming to the realization that a dream may be more than just a dream. It may be a genuine visit during which someone in spirit can share his or her energy and spend time with you. To fully experience the power of this kind of contact, you just need to open yourself to the possibility and tune in.

I've already mentioned some of my own dream encounters with my mother. They have been playful, joyful, loving, and expressive of her feelings, both happy ones and those of anger, as with my brother. They continue to fill me with the sense of peace and comfort that comes not only from our afterlife connection but also from knowing she's no longer suffering and seems once more healthy, witty, and having a good time—in other words, the way she was before her illness. One of her first dream messages came just two weeks after her death. In it she said, "I'm having a lot of fun," which immediately let me know that she was both free and doing her thing.

In the four years since her death, dream visits have been a constant vehicle for our transcommunication. To date, as I've recorded them in my journal, they number approximately 150. Knowing I can count on these visits has played a critical role in alleviating my grief. While they are a very different way of spending time together from what I experienced while she was alive, the bond we shared remains ever-present. Often when she visits, we are doing the same kinds of things we did in life—shopping, traveling, playing cards. Simple as they may seem, these shared pleasures continue to bring an emotional richness to my life.

Send an Invitation to Visit

If you haven't yet gotten a sign from your loved one, or if you haven't been aware of his or her presence, transcommunication can enable you to facilitate receiving a dream visit. By making a direct request or inviting your loved one to visit you in dreams, you will open the door to a vital and dynamic aspect of afterlife connection.

Because they are so personal and involve both visual and verbal interchange, dream visits have been, for me, among the most soul-nourishing ways I've found to continue my relationship with my mother. She's come to me without waiting for an actual invitation, probably because she's so certain the welcome mat will always be out. It's also possible however to ask for and receive, a dream visit if you haven't already received one without asking.

Later in this chapter, I'll suggest specific exercises you can use to create the mind-set and emotional climate most conducive to encouraging these visits, but first I'd like to talk a bit about why I think they're so healing and describe some of my own experiences, as well as those of my friends and patients.

Dream or Dream Visit—How Do You Know?

In my therapeutic work I'm highly attuned to the symbolic significance of dreams. I believe that one of the reasons dream visits play such a dominant role in our communications with the departed is closely related to the reasons that dreams in general can be so psychologically revealing. When we're sleeping, our ego— the pragmatic, analytical part of our personality—sleeps along with us and allows our subconscious spiritual energies to connect with and welcome what our logical, conscious mind cannot understand. In other words, there's no longer a little traffic cop standing guard at the crossroad and telling us what we should or should not accept as real or possible. Not only does this mean that those in spirit will have greater access to our psyche; it also means that it will be easier for us to accept the validity of the experience without being fearful. Dreams give us the opportunity, should we need to explain what we've experienced to ourselves, to rationalize the connection as the product of our own imagination. I suggest, however, that you not deprive yourself of the full value of what you've experienced by writing it off so easily.

Of course, not every dream we have about a loved one is an actual dream visit. For me, and for others with whom I've discussed them, dream visits have a particular interactive quality that sets them apart from ordinary dreams. We don't just dream about our loved ones; we're actually *in* the dream with them and usually participating in some form of activity we enjoyed together in the past. These visits have an intense reality that other dreams do not, and when we awaken from them, it's usually with a profound sense of love and well-being. That's why I encourage you, if you're keeping a connection catalog, to capture in your record not only what happened in your dream but also its emotional content— the feelings you had during the visit, the mood of your visiting loved one, and the emotions you experienced when you woke up. Remembering those feelings and emotions is one of the surest ways we have of distinguishing between a dream and an actual dream visit.

The way I distinguish between them is by the emotional impact of the experience. In a dream visit, you feel you are actually *with* your loved one. You feel his or her energy, and you share the experience completely. You are a participant—interacting, talking, laughing. You are a part of and involved in the moment, and it's an extremely powerful feeling. A dream, as opposed to a dream visit, is more like a narrative description than a dialogue. The person you're dreaming about is doing something, but you're not involved, you're not doing it with him. It's the interactive element that's key to the nature of a dream visit.

I remember a conversation I had with a friend not too long ago in which she described to me what she'd thought of as "just a dream." She'd spent the previous weekend at the home of her ex-sister-in-law, with whom she'd remained friendly after her own divorce. While she was there, she'd dreamed about her ex-father-in-law, who'd died about three years before. She described him to me "a real character" and "not the easiest man in the world," but "very interesting," and said that in the dream he was giving her a hard time just as he always used to do. Because she and her sister-in-law had been looking at old family photos earlier in the evening, it made a certain degree of sense to her that he would have been on her mind. And yet, she told me, she'd never dreamt about him before so far as she could remember.

I told her I thought she'd actually received a dream visit. In the dream she'd been laughing and interacting with her father-in-law, and the emotional content of the experience set it apart from an ordinary dream. At first she protested that she certainly didn't miss him and that he hadn't been a part of her life since she was divorced more than fifteen years before. But in the end she agreed that he had made a sentimental visit, since she was in his daughter's home, to let her know she was still in his world, and he in hers.

My friend Cynthia Richmond, a therapist and the author of *Dream Power,* shared with me one of her own emotional dream visits and the extraordinary manifestations that followed it.

She'd been driving cross-country with a friend when she received a phone call telling her that another beloved friend had died. Ed had been suffering from a form of emphysema and had caught a cold that turned into bronchitis. That night, she and her friend lit a candle and performed a little ritual of commemoration. Cynthia was sad both about losing her friend and about the fact that she hadn't been with him at the end. They'd planned to have dinner together shortly before she left on her trip, but she'd had to cancel at the last minute. She remembered the e-mail she'd sent: "We'll have plenty more times to get together soon." No one had expected Ed to die so suddenly, and now she was not only mourning but also feeling guilty. "We were buddies," she told me. "He was an incredible psychic, and he was both spiritual and scientific. We could talk about anything and everything, and we did."

During the night following the private commemoration ceremony she and her friend had held in a motel room somewhere between Los Angeles and Austin, Texas, Cynthia had a dream. In it, Ed, who was near seventy at the time of his death, appeared standing in battle fatigues and sang, "Your buddy misses you." Because she'd prayed and spoken to Ed's spirit in her own language before going to sleep, Cynthia wasn't entirely surprised by her dream. "Still," she said, "it was so vivid. I knew he had actually come to me to let me know there were no hard feelings and that he valued my friendship as I had his."

Ed's family had asked her to speak at his funeral, and Cynthia had agreed to cut her trip short and fly back to L.A. First however, she felt she needed to complete the drive to Austin with her friend, who would be starting a new job and was nervous about driving alone. Cynthia didn't feel right about abandoning her and decided that, if she got on a plane as soon as they arrived in Austin, she could still be back in time for the funeral. What happened next confirmed the fact that she'd made the right decision. The following morning, she and her traveling companion got back in their car to continue their drive. Cynthia put a Chet Baker CD she'd just bought into the car's CD player. There on the stereo was Chet singing "My Buddy," a World War II song about a soldier who loses his buddy in battle. "It sent chills down my spine," Cynthia told me. "I just smiled and looked up and said, 'Okay, buddy, I'll be there.'" But it didn't end yet.

A few months later, she was in her living room reading *Divine Secrets of the Ya-Ya Sisterhood*. Near the end of the book, the Ya-Yas sing a song. There in front of her were printed the lyrics to

"My Buddy." Cynthia said that her eyes filled with tears. She felt a warmth in her chest and an ache in her stomach at the same time. She looked up from the book to blink away the tears, and there, behind the couch she'd been lying on, she saw movement, "like vibrating molecules in the shape of a man!" The last time Ed was at her house, he had paused behind the couch to catch his breath and had carried on a conversation with her from that very spot. Cynthia said she'd felt compelled to sing him the song. So, reading the words from the book, she did just that. By the end of the song, she'd closed her eyes, and, when she opened them again, the moving air was gone. "There wasn't a single doubt in my mind," she said, "that I'd shared a loving exchange with my friend—he in the spirit world, I in the physical."

Toni Robino, the writer to whom my mother introduced herself so dramatically in chapter 1, also told me about a dream visit paid to her by her father, in which his manner and means of expression were so vivid and so true to life that she knew it was more than a dream. It occurred on the night of the day he was buried. Toni dreamt that she was walking in the halls of Trump Tower in Manhattan, opening doors and looking for her good friend, who actually lived there. When she opened one particular door, she saw her father kneeling over a person who appeared to be dying and saying, "Don't worry, I know you're scared now but in a few minutes you're going to be in the light; it's going to be fine; I'm going to be with you the entire time."

"Dad, what are you doing here?" Toni asked.

"I'm doing my job. What did you think I'd be doing, just sitting around?" he replied. It was, Toni said, "exactly the way he communicated in life.

"I believe they [our departed loved ones] try to communicate with us in various ways," she told me, "and some of them may be better at it than others. We need to look for nonverbal cues because not all of us are equally verbal.

"Some dreams are just like a computer tape backup of what's happened in our day, but certain dreams actually seem to be happening in real time. This one was so clear, so vivid, and my dad's personality was so much him, that I knew it was a dream visit. It was very comforting and really validated what I'd always believed to be true—that we can communicate with the departed."

The emotional wallop packed by some of my own dream visits has been so electrifying that it still makes the hair on my arms stand on end. The first of these occurred just about six months after my mother's death, and this is how I described it in my journal: "You 'plugged' in. The wires lit up bright green, and I knew you were online." I remember that I felt as if a phone line had suddenly been electrified. I heard my mother's voice exquisitely clearly, and we spoke of our love for one another and how difficult the separation had been for both of us. The following morning, I wrote, "You were really there." The feeling I had of our connecting and declaring both our love and our pain was indescribably intense.

Several months later she called on the phone again. "I was plugged in to you," I wrote in my journal. "My hair tingled, and we had a phenomenal ordinary conversation." At the end, she said, "Don't tell anyone," and I thanked her for being with me. Interestingly, I had recorded this in my journal as having occurred on May 2. It wasn't until I was rereading my connection catalog in the course of writing this book that I realized it had actually happened after midnight—on May 3, the anniversary of her death.

Yet another of what I've come to think of as my plugged-in dream visits took place about a year later. In the dream, my phone rang, and, when I picked it up, my mother and father were each on separate extensions, which is exactly how we used to talk. This time she must have decided not to keep it a secret because we carried on a three-way conversation that I knew was absolutely real. Somewhere in the dream a green light flashed on, as if to alert me or "turn me on" to the fact that this was actually happening. Interestingly, it was the same bright green as the light that had appeared in her first phone visit the year before. It wasn't just a dream *about* a phone conversation. I was actually *in* that conversation. The difference may be difficult to describe in so many words, but the feeling when it happens is unmistakable.

Because my mother lived in Florida and I in New York, the way we kept up our constant communication was mainly by telephone, which may be the reason this is now one of her preferred modes of connecting. I also believe, however, that telephones, which are transmitters of energy, naturally become vehicles for afterlife connections. So, my mother is still on the line, albeit from an even-longer distance.

Many people—even those who might accept the possibility of actual dream visits—dismiss the notion that animals, too, have an afterlife and can continue to communicate with us after death. Nevertheless, one of the most touching recent examples of how dream communications can relieve our sadness and sense of loss involved a friend of mine who'd been mourning the death of her beloved springer spaniel, Tess. Tess's great friend had been Buzz, a beautiful golden retriever who passed several years before her. Tess and Buzz had loved running on the beach at Fire Island, leaping over the dunes and chasing the deer they never managed to catch. My friend told me at dinner one evening that she'd dreamed about Tess and Buzz the night before and that they'd both been healthy and full of energy, running after deer as neither of them could do at the end of their lives. I asked her how she felt when she woke up, and she told me she'd felt peaceful and happy, much less sad than she had for a long time. I knew then that what she'd experienced was much more than a dream I told her that I thought Tess and Buzz had paid her a visit to let her know that they *were* happy and still playing together and that she didn't have to worry about them anymore.

Yet another way of knowing that a dream is actually a dream visit is to receive information we didn't have previously and wouldn't know how to access. In his book, *Messages and Miracles,* Louis E. LaGrand refers to what is, historically, one of the best-documented of these cases. It seems that for months after his death, Dante's sons had been searching his house, trying to find the final section of the manuscript for *The Divine Comedy.* Then one night, Jacob, one of the sons, dreamed that his father appeared before him dressed all in white. In his dream Jacob asked his father if he'd finished the poem. Dante nodded yes, and, still in the dream, he led his son to the place where he'd secreted the manuscript. The next day Jacob called upon his father's attorney, and together they went to the place Dante had pointed out. There, behind a small window, they found the missing papers covered with mold.

Another, equally remarkable example is the dream in which Samuel Taylor Coleridge received the words to one of his best-known poems, "Kubla Khan." Afterwards, Coleridge wrote of the experience, referring to himself in the third person.

> In the summer of the year 1797, the Author, then in ill health, had retired to a lonely farm-house between Porlock and Linton. . . . In consequence of a slight indisposition, an anodyne had been prescribed, from the effects of which he fell asleep in his chair at the moment that he was reading the following sentence, or words of the same substance, in *Purchas's Pilgrimage*: "Here the Khan Kubla commanded a palace to be built, and a stately garden thereunto. And thus ten miles of fertile ground were inclosed [sic] with a wall." The Author continued for about three hours in a profound sleep, at least of the external senses, during which time he has the most vivid confidence that he could not have composed less than from two to three hundred lines; if that indeed can be called composition in which all the images rose up before him as *things,* with a parallel production of the correspondent expressions, without any sensation or consciousness of effort. On awakening he appeared to himself to have a distinct recollection of the whole, and taking his pen, ink, and paper, instantly and eagerly wrote down the lines that are here preserved.

Unfortunately, Coleridge was called away before he could transcribe the entire poem, and when he returned, all but a fragment "had passed away like the images on the surface of a stream into which a stone has been cast . . ."

Some might say, of course, that Coleridge had simply experienced a form of literary inspiration, that the poem came from his own subconscious rather than from the world of spirit, and that is certainly one explanation. However, it's also possible to speculate that the very source of that kind of inspiration *is* the world of spirit. Either way, the poet himself considered it an extraordinary experience beyond rational explanation.

On a more contemporary note, Renee, the patient with whom I was talking when our mothers disconnected our call, has also described to me a dream visit from her grandmother in which she heard words in a language that she didn't understand and, therefore, could never have "dreamed up" on her own.

Renee's grandmother was ninety-five when she died. She'd been living with her daughter, Renee's mother, who was also seriously ill at the time, as was Renee's husband, David. Renee had been trying to hold her emotions in check but had at one point broken down and confessed to her mother, "I'm so scared. You're so sick, and David's so sick. I'm so frightened for both of you."

With that, Renee's mother had looked at her and said, "David's going to be fine, you'll see. I'm going to go, but he'll be fine."

"I didn't want her to know how upset I was," Renee said. "I didn't want her to feel that she had to take care of *me*. Part of me understood that she knew. I'd always believed and trusted everything she told me, so it was tremendously comforting to know that David would live, yet so painful to think of losing her. When I told him what she'd said, he just nodded and agreed, 'I'll be fine.'"

A week after Renee's grandmother died, she came to her in a dream, looking happy, healthy, and far younger than her ninety-five years. "I was so happy to see her," Renee told me. "I kept saying, 'Grandma, you look great! How are you?'" But her only response was to keep repeating, *"Tochter, tochter,"* a word Renee didn't understand, although she assumed it was Yiddish.

The next day, when she described the dream to her, Renee's

mother began to weep as she explained that the word was indeed the Yiddish word for "daughter." "She's calling for me," said Renee's mother. "She's waiting for me to join her." It was a validation of her earlier prediction, and it was exactly what came to pass. Renee's husband, who'd been suffering from a very advanced stage of colon cancer, amazingly recovered fully while her mother sadly died.

Don't Let Them Slip Away

While every individual night visit can be comforting, exhilarating, healing, and more I've found that, when I look back through my connection catalog, I see sequences of events that I didn't recognize as they were happening.

One of the primary reasons I started keeping my journal was that, like all dreams, my mother's visits had a habit of slipping away from me shortly after I awakened, so I wanted to write them down before I forgot them. Sometimes I even found that the very act of recording one of these dreams brought back details I hadn't remembered until I actually started to write. In addition, simply accumulating the data showed me how often a dream visit was followed by one or more additional forms of manifestation the next day. Eventually the mere volume of dreams and the events that surrounded them made it clear to me beyond any doubt that what I was experiencing was real and not to be dismissed as merely wishful thinking or coincidence.

Most often, I've found, a dream visit is the prelude to some kind of electronic or mechanical failure. In fact, this has happened so often that I now find it not only comforting but also amusing to know why so many of my appliances go on the fritz. My personal belief about all such breakage is that the person in spirit brings an enormous amount of energy to the dream visit, and when the visit ends, there's a residue of energy still on this plane that causes the electronic disturbances.

I remember, for example, one particularly vivid dream encounter in which my father was telling me how much he loved my mother. I knew that my mother was there, too, and that she'd come back to get a little more love. The next morning, as I was drying my hair, I was thinking about all the electrical problems I'd been having, and saying silently to her, "Boy, it sure is good to know that when things break, it's you saying hello, because otherwise it could really be very irritating." No sooner had the thought passed through my mind than my hair dryer began blowing cold air. No matter what setting I tried, it continued to blow cold. I had to laugh because the hair dryer's breaking would ordinarily have annoyed me no one. But because I'd just spoken to my mother, letting her know that I understood what was going on, I was amused and—believe it or not—thankful; I felt she was validating my message to her. At that point I just said out loud to her, "I knew you'd be here today after the dream visit I had last night!"

Sometimes the signs our loved ones send us can be truly annoying—like Charlie's being awakened by the blue jays, the air-conditioning in Josie's car going dead, and my brother's being plunged into darkness—until we come to realize their significance. Then they take on a whole new meaning, and our annoyance dissolves into appreciation, even amusement. It sometimes seems as if they actually choose to annoy us in order to make sure that they're getting our attention.

Virtually the same sequence—a dream visit followed by a loss of power—has happened so often that by now I've actually lost count. Not all these nighttime adventures are precursers to breakage. They have also been followed by my seeing a butterfly, hearing "La Vie en Rose," or becoming aware of presence in some other way. One evening following a dream visit, for example, I was lying in bed and randomly flipped on the television, tuning in to just the right station at just the right moment to see Katerina Witt skating to "La Vie en Rose." Also, the night before that Father's Day, when my dad opened his present just as that very song began playing on the radio, I'd had a dream visit in which my mother let me know she was "sleeping quite a bit and healing." Over and over in my journal, I note dream visits followed by some other validating signal. Only by looking back do I see that these multiple manifestations very often occur on special occasions or anniversaries.

Reconsidering my mother's visits in tranquility as I page through my journal has also allowed me to see other kinds of connections and meanings I didn't recognize at the time. In one visit, for example she and I were going somewhere (I'm not sure where). She was trying to leave, and we were looking for a door when she said to me, "Look for the human exit." Then, just two nights later, she came to me again, and this time when she spoke to me, she said, quite distinctly, "Baby, you better believe it." That happens to have been one of her favorite expressions, but at the time I didn't know what it was she was telling me I'd better believe.

It wasn't until I looked back at those two entries that I was struck by their true meaning and by the implication of their proximity. It now seems to me that this was the first time I'd crossed over into the realm of spirit and that my mother was telling me to "look for the human exit" so that I could return to my body on the earthly plane. I also believe that her saying, "you better believe it," just two nights later was intended to make sure that I believed she was really there. As I've already said, if we're not tuned in to the spiritual messages we receive, it's possible for us to gloss over whatever our loved ones are trying to convey. Keeping a written record can enrich the meaning of these messages by providing us with the opportunity to reflect upon them at a later time.

Do they come to us, or do we go to them, or do we meet somehow on neutral spiritual turf? It's hard to say when we're awake and limited by our physical bodies within the confines of time and space. But I do believe that on at least that one occasion, my spirit did cross over, and that my mother was helping me get back. Both the belief and the possibility were echoed by one of my patients not so long ago when she told me about a dream she'd had about her brothers, Timmy and Johnny, both of whom were tragically killed in the World Trade Center, where they worked just one floor apart. Carolee told me that when they were growing up, her brothers had done everything together while always excluding her. She'd frequently begged them to let her go along but invariably wound up being left behind and feeling left out. Now, she said to me, with more than a touch of bitterness, "Can you believe the irony? They've really left me behind again." She said that one night she was in a dead sleep—a luxury she rarely enjoyed because she normally woke up several times during the night—when she dreamt that her two brothers were standing outside a limousine, getting ready to go somewhere. By way of preface to this story, Carolee told me that, except for three grandparents, there had been no significant deaths in her family until July of 1999, when her aunt Ginny died. Then, in 2000 her one remaining grandmother, Mary, and an uncle both died. In 2001 she had a miscarriage and lost both her brothers, and Ronnie, another uncle who was also her godfather, died as well. It was during the night following the day of her uncle Ronnie's death that she had this dream.

Timmy and Johnny, she said, were laughing and having fun. "There was a crowd of people waiting in the car, and I wanted to go with them, but they wouldn't let me. Finally, I got so annoyed that I got in my van and drove off thinking, 'Once more they've left me out.'"

She awakened the next morning feeling "remarkably jubilant and happy." Even though, in the dream, she'd been annoyed at being left out, when she woke up, she realized the true significance of what had occurred. "I knew with certainty that I had left my body that night. I knew I had seen them all. Everyone in that car was someone in my family who'd died, and that's why I couldn't go with them. It made me happy to know they were all together and that they were still with me—that I hadn't really been left behind."

Open Your Mind to Their Spirit

Keeping your connection catalog is one way to help ensure these precious visits aren't lost to you in waking life, but first you have to recognize and accept their validity.

Gloria, a patient of mine, received dream visits from her grandmother that she might have dismissed entirely if it hadn't been for a phone-therapy session we had just a couple of weeks after her grandmother's death. She was lying in a hammock as we talked, telling me about the extremely close and trusting relationship she'd had with her grandmother, saying that she'd never been afraid to state whatever was on her mind.

Then, suddenly, she exclaimed, "Jane, a butterfly has actually just landed on my arm." And then, just a few seconds later, "Oh, my goodness, would you look at that? Two rabbits just came out of the woods and hopped right over to me. I've never, ever seen them come out of the woods before."

As all this was happening, I said to her, "Gloria, that's your grandmother coming through to you." To me, the butterfly and the two rabbits were signs that couldn't be missed because they're just the ones my mother so often sends to me. After saying that, I immediately asked if she'd dreamed about her grandmother recently. That's when she told me about the following two dream visits, the second of which had occurred just the night before.

The first one took place just a week or so after her grandmother died. In it, she appeared floating upside down in a mirror. "Why don't you come down out of the mirror," Gloria asked her, at which point her grandmother thrust a hand out toward her. "Won't you please come out?" Gloria asked again. "I don't like communicating in symbols." On that occasion Gloria's grandmother did not come out to clarify her message. She did, however, make a return visit just the night before our telephone session. Upon seeing her this second time, Gloria had said, "Grandma, I thought you were dead."

"I'm not dead," her grandmother replied.

After hearing about her dreams, I suggested to Gloria that, since her grandmother was clearly connecting so strongly with her, she start to keep a journal of these kinds of events. She told me afterwards that the realization of her grandmother's continuing presence in her life had done much to mitigate the depth of her loss. I encourage you, as I did Gloria, to embrace the validity of dream visits so that you, too, can profit from the kind of comfort she has found.

The "I'm not dead" dream that Gloria had is one that, I've discovered, many people experience. I believe that, in dream visits of this kind, our loved ones are letting us know, in most dramatic fashion, that their spirit and energy—the very essence of who they are—lives on, and so, in the most profound and spiritual sense, they are not dead.

I myself have had just this kind of visit from my mother on more than one occasion. In her "I'm not dead" visits, she lets me know that she is, indeed quite alive and well, albeit on another plane. Each time one occurs, I'm left with a feeling of pure joy and amazement.

My patient Angie, who experienced the mysterious appearance of the ABF truck on a deserted highway after her brother-in-law's death, has also told me of dream visits he's paid to her sister and of her concern that her sister was letting their significance slip away. In the first visit he said, "See, honey, everything's okay; nothing's changed; I'm still here." In another, they were sitting in a swing eating ice cream (which is something they'd done all the time), and again he said, "I just want you to know I'm okay here."

Angie told me that her sister had at first been very reluctant to acknowledge either the fact that Eric was still with her in spirit or that she had been visited by his presence. This had been very frustrating for Angie, who was open to all kinds of psychic phenomena, but she'd persisted in encouraging her sister to accept the messages that were coming through to her as dream visits. Gradually, Angie told me, her sister did come to accept the possibility of afterlife connection and acknowledged that, although it was still a bit scary, it made her feel "a hundred percent better" to know that Eric was okay.

Not too long ago, while Angie was nervously awaiting the results of a medical test, Eric once more came to her sister in a dream visit, looking fine and healthy and telling her that he was taking a new job much closer to home. Her sister woke up the next morning feeling great. By this time she was tuned into the significance of her dream visits and called Angie to share the experience and let her know she was sure that Eric had been telling her Angie was going to be fine. Sure enough, that very day Angie received a call from her doctor with the good news that the results of her test were indeed negative.

If you yourself have overcome doubts, but others around you are still closed, keep trying to encourage them to be open, because your faith can help them come around, as Angie's did for her sister. Their acceptance of what is spiritually possible can ultimately be as healing for them as it has been for you.

In Agee's *A Death in the Family,* when the Follets are gathered on the evening after Jay's death, the women of the family all sense his presence in the house. When Mary Follet's skeptical father questions her belief in the survival of the soul, her only answer is, "It takes faith, Papa." Mary's faith stems from her strong religious convictions, but I would suggest that, whatever its source, all any of us needs to access the world of spirit is an openness of mind and the faith of heart that it is available to us.

They Want to Communicate

While it may take faith on our part, I believe that our loved ones in spirit know just how important it can be for us to hear from them, and that they'll leave no stone unturned to be sure their message is delivered. Carol, a good friend of mine, reinforced this conviction when she told me about two dream visits her sister, Meg, had paid to a close friend of hers.

Carol's friend, Beth, had never even met Meg, but knew her only through Carol. She received her first visit on the night Meg died after a long and painful illness. Carol had been with her at the hospital all the previous day, rubbing her arms and talking softly. Every once in a while Carol said, Meg would open her eyes and say, "Oh, that feels so good. That's so nice what you're doing."

"And I kept rubbing her arms," Carol went on. "I told her she was the best sister I ever could have had. We said everything that could be said."

That night, Beth dreamt that she and Meg were together. "Her feet were enormous, so swollen. I spent my dream night working on her feet, massaging them, kind of holding them. At the end, her feet were back to normal size. They were fine, beautiful."

When Beth awakened, she knew she had to tell Carol about the dream, but before she had a chance to call her, Carol phoned to say Meg had died during the night. "For me," Beth told me, "it was the chill of, 'Oh my goodness!' After the funeral, I shared my dream with Carol. I think it made her happy knowing that Meg was a little more comfortable."

"It was amazing," Carol agreed, "to think that Beth could have gotten so close to what was actually happening. And her feet being back to normal size—that let me know she had somehow made the transition. It was remarkable."

Beth's second dream visit came about two months later. In the dream, Beth was in her office, which was divided into small bays with low dividers, so that it was possible to see one's co-workers in adjacent cubicles. In a cubicle adjacent to hers, she saw Meg talking on the phone. "Meg, I can't believe you're here," she said. At that point, Meg put her hand over the phone, leaned toward Beth, and said, "Tell Carol I'm okay."

"It was very clear," Beth told me. "She was saying, 'Let her know I'm fine.' She looked beautiful. She had a full, beautiful head of hair, and there was a lot of white light around her."

"It was very gratifying," Carol explained, "because I hadn't been looking for messages. I just remember thinking, *Isn't it wonderful that Meg is sending me a message?*"

Although Beth didn't know Meg, she'd been a friend of Carol's for many years, and she was more attuned to the spiritual world than Carol. "My background or inclination is very Jungian," she told me. "So, for me, dreams are a particularly strong window into the soul and into the other side." As a result, she's sure Meg chose her as the person most likely to deliver her message in a way that ensured Carol would really hear it.

Two other such roundabout connections were made by the parents of my patient, Michele, whose many remarkable messages from both her mother and her father I told you about in the previous chapter. Michele's mother first came to her through a woman in her office who had never met her mother but had seen pictures of her on Michele's desk. My patient told me that her mother had come to her coworker in a dream just about three weeks after her death, ringing the doorbell in the middle of a dinner party. The woman, in her dream, opened the door to find her standing on the porch, beautifully dressed and carrying a suitcase. She was clearly able to walk, which she hadn't been for several months prior to her death. "Mrs. K., what are you doing here?" the astonished woman asked. "I'm very tired. I'm going to sit down for a while. It's been a long journey," was Mrs. K.'s response. When Michele told me this story, she explained that her mother had always loved parties but that she'd been bedridden before her death. Getting this message through her coworker was tremendously comforting because she felt that her mother was telling her she was now back to her party-going self and no longer in pain.

I agreed, adding that I believed Michele's mother was letting her know that her transition to the spirit world was complete and that she was now ready to connect with her daughter.

A similar third-party message was delivered after the death of Michele's father, sometime after her mother died. In this case, she received a phone call at work from Tom Trotta, a psychic who lives down the street from her family. Tom frequently met her father when they were both buying groceries in the local Stop & Shop. "How's your dad?" he asked. When Michele told him her father had died the week before, he gasped, "Oh, my God, that's why he came through in my dream." He then proceeded to share his dream with her. "His face was glowing," Tom said. "Now it makes sense. He was dead. That's why his face was glowing. 'Marty,' I said to him, 'I'll see you at the Stop & Shop.' 'I'm not gonna be there anymore,' he told me. Then he said, 'You've never been to my pool, and I want you to call my daughter.' So that's why I was calling you."

"I'd been so down," Michele said. "That call brought me so up. I was so relieved. It eased the loneliness, and I really felt empowered for a couple of days."

I told Michele I believed her father was glowing because he and her mother were together on the other side, and that they wanted her to know that. Our loved ones want us to know they are well and happy because they understand knowing that will help us to heal.

Protective Messages from the Spirit World

As I've said, most dream visits find us engaging with our loved ones in activities we once enjoyed in the flesh, which is why they leave us with a lingering sense of peace and joy. Sometimes, however, our guardian angels also deliver advance warnings of difficult or dangerous times to come.

One of the clearest, most startling examples I've ever heard of this kind of message was told to me by Renee, whose mother had earlier predicted her own death. After her mother died, Renee had communicated with her spirit for several years, then she became pregnant with her first child. It was during the seventh month of her pregnancy that Renee's mother made a dream visit different from any Renee had received from her in the past. This time, she appeared in a door frame surrounded by a pitch-black background. "I was happy to see her," Renee told me, "but she'd never appeared like that before."

"Mom, it's great to see you," she said. "I've been wanting to tell you, I'm having a baby. You're going to be a grandmother. Aren't you excited?"

But Renee's mother seemed very serious and didn't answer her.

"Mom, didn't you hear me?" Renee persisted. "You're going to have a grandchild."

When she finally spoke, all her mother said was, "Be prepared."

When Renee awoke the next morning, she told her husband about her weird dream. Even though he simply chalked it up to her anxiety about giving birth without her mother there and told her to forget about it, Renee said, "I couldn't forget about it. It made me uneasy. Her reaction was so serious. It was very disturbing. It was out of character for her, and it wasn't the way I would have dreamt about her; I would have dreamt about her the way she was—her personality when she was alive. Part of me wanted to agree with David. But part of me knew it was more than just a dream."

Renee went into labor the following month and gave birth to a stillborn child. Afterward she said, "My mother obviously knew what I was going to be dealing with, and she protected me by helping me to prepare for it." Being alerted in that way, she said, brought her comfort because she understood that her mother was still watching over her. Fortunately Renee went on to have other, healthy children. She still enjoys meaningful dream visits from her mother, who has continued to be a constant and caring guide.

Another such warning was reported by my friend Lisa, who had a dream in which her mother let her know that she'd seen her being hit by a car. The very next day, Lisa was driving in the car with her granddaughter. When they pulled to the curb, the child immediately started to climb out the street-side door. Because of her dream, Lisa reached over, pulled the door shut, and told her to get out on the curb side. Just at that moment, a truck hit their car from behind, and both Lisa and her granddaughter were thrown onto the lawn. Had they been on the other side of the car, she told me, they both surely would have been killed. "Thank God my mother came through in that dream!" she exclaimed. "She saved our lives!"

Our guardians in spirit can prepare us for what's to come, and they can alert us to possibilities that may—if we're able to hear them—allow us to make better decisions than we might otherwise have made. By doing that they can help us to avoid what might be harmful or destructive. They can also, as I'll be discussing in later chapters, put people and opportunities in our path that will allow us to heal and make better choices for ourselves in the future.

Facilitating Conscious Contact in the Dream World

Although dream visits are among the most frequent and meaningful ways those in spirit have of communicating with us, it's possible that you haven't yet experienced one, or, if you have, that you want to increase the frequency of those you do receive. Possibly you've already been visited by your loved one but were not aware enough at the time to recognize the fact that what your were experiencing was more than just a dream.

I myself have experienced what I've come to call "flash visits," which are really just fleeting experiences of my mother's presence during which she comes and goes from my dream in a flash. I know she's there, but the encounter is not of the same magnitude or emotional depth as a full-blown dream visit. Yet it's still a visit because I'm distinctly aware of her presence.

If any of these scenarios applies to you, there are steps you can take to open yourself up more fully to the possibilities of transcommunication and increase both the frequency and meaning of the visits you receive.

To facilitate your dream visits, I suggest you harness your psychic energy and power-up your receptivity by practicing this simple "Soul Mind-set" exercise.

1. When you're ready to settle down for the night, sit in a comfortable chair or on your bed and clear your mind of the problems and concerns of the day by doing the "Sign Language" meditation on pages 138–140.
2. Once you're feeling relaxed and calm, invite your loved one to visit by saying out loud, "I'm ready to see you now," if you haven't already experienced a visit. Or, "I'm ready to see you again. I'd welcome a visit from you tonight." Then, if you wish, you can reinforce your invitation by lighting a candle or reciting a simple prayer composed of feelings or thoughts that are particularly meaningful to you.
3. Now that your invitation has been sent, go to sleep with the understanding that you've done all you can to initiate

contact and release the unconscious energy that will allow the contact to occur. Taking these steps won't necessarily guarantee that your loved one will come to you that night, but if the conditions are right, you may well receive a meaningful visit from the spirit world.

Cynthia Richmond suggests adding even more power to your ritual of invitation by holding or looking at an object that belonged to your loved one, something that brings back pleasant memories and provides you with a feeling of closeness. A photograph, a piece of jewelry you remember your loved one wore, or any personal object, she says, can help to draw his or her energy near.

"I've always felt my grandmother near," she told me. "In fact, whenever I misplace something, I sit down, take a deep breath, and ask, 'Grandma Rachel, where did I leave my keys?'—or whatever it is I've lost. Nearly every time I get a clear picture of a location, and that's where I find my missing item.

"Sometime ago, I was involved in a difficult relationship, and I really wanted to talk things over with my grandmother. I was so sad that day, feeling sorry for myself because I was having to navigate my way through life without her wise advice. I'd taken her recipe box from the cupboard and looked at every card in it. I traced her handwriting with my finger and remembered the delicious meals she used to make and the funny stories we would share as we did the dishes together after dinner. Several times, I closed my eyes and held the box close to my heart as I took a brief trip down my own memory lane." Cynthia said that after she went to sleep that night, she awakened knowing that her grandmother was there, holding her hands. "My eyes were still closed," she told me. "I felt my grandma's small, worn hands holding mine, and they were warm. Grandma was a seamstress and a gardener. She sewed for all her grandchildren and had a rose garden she was very proud of, but all that hard work had taken a toll on her hands. She had swollen, arthritic knuckles and raised veins. Her hands were unmistakable." Cynthia looked directly into my eyes as she shared her experience. She wanted me to know exactly how she'd felt. "I somehow knew that if I opened my eyes she would go away, but, at the same time, I was desperate to see her. Very slowly, I opened my eyes, and just as gently she released her grip and was gone. I'll never forget it. She knew I needed her, and she showed me that she was there for me. Since that time, I've had many talks with her. I just relax, close my eyes, and bring her to mind, and we have a chat. I feel that very often I hear the advice she would have given me if she were actually sitting with me. Sometimes she just makes me laugh."

Cynthia also says that dream visits are the best vehicle for departed loved ones to come to you simply because they're not as scary as if a spirit just materialized before your eyes in a waking state. Do take her suggestion for using a physical object as a way to enhance the energy of your invitation.

Adding Value to Your Visits

All dream visits are valuable simply because they are links in an ever-growing chain of continued communication, the dots and dashes of your spiritual Morse code. It's also possible, however, to enhance their value by influencing and focusing their content in order to receive answers to your questions or to resolve issues you and your loved one might not have been able to deal with when he or she was alive. If you want or need to do that, it's up to you to shape and structure the content of the dream, because those who have passed no longer have the same issues with us that we might have with them. They have no agenda except to let us know that they're still with us and that we still have their love.

If you want to know something specific, you have to ask the question, but even doing that won't *guarantee* you'll get the answer you're looking for. Your departed loved one may respond, but not necessarily to what's on your mind. When that happens, you must first pay attention to the message he or she has sent you. The one in spirit may want you to "get it" before you get the answer you want. There are, however, some steps you can take to improve your chances of receiving the information you seek.

1. Complete the "Sign Language" meditation on pages 138–140 and invite your loved one to visit.
2. Either in writing or out loud, ask him or her for guidance with whatever specific issue may have been troubling you or that you need to clarify.
3. Go to sleep, allowing the power of the unconscious to unfold so that the contact can occur.

As I've been saying all along, our loved ones still love us. Because of that, if they are able to, they *will* provide the guidance we need to make good decisions and achieve positive growth for ourselves.

In addition to asking the questions that might enable you to resolve troubling issues, you can also facilitate the completion of a previous message that may have been incomplete or unclear. Dreams of all kinds can seem confusing or cryptic simply because their language is so often symbolic. They can also be so fragmentary that we awaken with the feeling that there was more to be said. That can be far more frustrating than getting cut off for no apparent reason in the middle of a phone call. It's possible, though, to "redial" the spirit world and try to complete the conversation. I encourage you to commit yourself to the process, have faith, and above all keep a journal of some kind that will allow you to see how the puzzle pieces are coming together.

I've already told you about dream visits from my mother whose significance became apparent to me only after I'd gone back to review the notes I'd made in my journal, as well as those linked events whose relationship I didn't immediately recognize. If you've been keeping a connection catalog of your own, you might find, either at the time of recording a dream or at some later date, that you're not quite sure about the meaning of the message. In that case, take the following steps.

Clear the static from your mind by doing your meditation; boost the power of your invitation by holding or looking at an object as Cynthia Richmond suggests; review the dream you would like to continue, making the details as clear as possible in your mind's eye; and then ask your loved one for the clarification you hope to receive. Frame the issue in your mind, focus your thoughts, and ask aloud for the answer to your question.

I'm sure we've all, at one time or another, awakened from a dream that was so pleasant or so incomplete that we wished we could continue it. If we're lucky—if the alarm isn't demanding that we get up and get going—sometimes we're able to do just that. Well, the same possibility exists for continuing a dream visit inadvertently cut short. Perhaps your visitor didn't have enough psychic energy to stay any longer. Or perhaps your own psychic reservoir ran dry. There's no reason why, after your visitor has recharged his or her batteries or you've refilled the pool, you shouldn't be able to complete the communication.

A Visit Is a Visit—Even If It's "Only" a Dream

Hearing songs, seeing birds, butterflies, rainbows, or rabbits, even breakage and electronic blowouts, once we recognize them as varieties of afterlife connection, can be happy reminders of an ongoing communication with our loved ones in spirit. To me, however, dream visits are among the most profound connections of all. They actually allow us to spend some time with those whose physical presence we've been missing and whom we may have thought would be lost to us forever. They even enable us to engage in meaningful dialogues that can be both heartwarming and healing.

My impetus for writing this book and sharing not only my own very personal experiences but also those of others who've agreed to let me tell their stories has always been to help others enjoy the emotional healing that comes through our ability to communicate with the spirit world. Philosophers and poets have long speculated about survival of consciousness, professional mediums have demonstrated and written about their special powers, and men of science have tried to prove that spiritual energy doesn't die. My own continuing connection with my mother, particularly our encounters in the world of dreams, has made it abundantly clear to me that every single one of us can access spiritual energy. If we are willing to set aside our skepticism and welcome the adventure, we can actively initiate contacts that will be therapeutic and will empower us with a sense of continuing love and support. Our feelings of abandonment are alleviated, we feel less alone, and our grief is mitigated by the knowledge that our loved one is still very much alive in spirit and is protecting us from the other side.

I urge you, therefore, to take the steps I've provided here for

Part Three

The Healing
Connection

6.

Writing from the Heart— Letters to the Spirit Realm

Good thoughts bear good fruit, bad thoughts bear bad fruit—and man is his own gardener.

—JAMES ALLEN

Writing is a powerful tool that can work for us on several levels. I've already shared with you how valuable and sustaining it has been for me to keep my connection catalog, but there are many other ways writing can help you to facilitate conscious contact.

The Power of Channeled Writing

Channeled writing is a way to connect with a being in spirit by putting oneself into a meditative or self-induced hypnotic state and letting the words just flow onto the paper without conscious thought.

I was personally introduced to the powers of channeled writing by Maria Papapetros, the psychic with whom I've worked professionally. Maria lost her son, Randy, in 1981, when he was a teenager, and she now receives much of her information from his spirit through channeled writing.

After his death Maria was using journaling as a way of recording and working through her feelings. One day, as she was writing, a letter came through from Randy saying, "Start writing to me. I'm going to prove to you that it's me." She took that to mean that he would offer some form of confirmation that the messages she was receiving through her writings were coming from him.

Despite her own psychic abilities, Maria was initially skeptical of what she saw appearing on the page—she was operating in this instance as a mother who'd lost a child, not as a professional psychic. Confirmation did come, however, through the friends and other people to whom she showed his letters. Each of these people to his or her amazement felt that the message he or she read had been intended specifically for him or her. That, in fact, is one of the most interesting aspects of the information Randy supplies in his letters. They are always relevant and make sense to the person who's reading one. The same is true for Maria. Whenever she rereads one at random, no matter when it was written, it is relevant to the time she's reading it. Maria and Randy have been writing for many years now, and the information he provides is uncannily accurate in ways that defy the boundaries of time and space.

For example, here is an excerpt from a letter Maria received from him on September 8, 1996, that is remarkably predictive of events surrounding September 11, 2001:

I see a big mountains [sic] colliding. Two big mountains are going to meet. It may be the East and the West. And then, after the collision, there will be peace. I see George rising again. There will be more wars. A king from the Middle East called maybe Massoud will rule, and he'll rule wisely. Ang [sic] then, the wars will cease.

Those who work professionally with the world of spirit will tell you that on the spiritual plane the boundaries of time and space no longer exist, which is why the information Randy provides, and that psychics provide their clients, may not seem relevant at the moment but will come true at some other time and in some other place.

Maria's assistant, Neal, recently told me of having just this kind of timeless experience when he misplaced a number of letters Maria had given him and didn't want to ask her for duplicate copies. In the midst of his search, he went out to dinner with a friend he hadn't seen in a year, and when he returned home afterwards, he suddenly knew exactly where he'd put them. He went directly to the place where they'd been buried under a pile of other papers and pulled them out. Then he said to himself, "Let's just see what Randy has to say," and took one out at random. It was dated 1988—many years before—and began, "Happy Birthday Phyllis. We both wish you a happy birthday. Mom tells me you are fine I know you are fine. . . ." Even Neal was amazed to realize that it was Phyllis, the very same Phyllis referred to in the letter, with whom he'd just had dinner.

Neal said that on yet another occasion, back in 1984, Maria had told him that Randy was going to contact him. "Sure, sure," he'd said to himself. Yet, when he called his answering service later that day (at that time he didn't have an answering machine), the woman running the service told him there was a message in his box with a phone number but no name. She said she didn't remember when it was received or how it had gotten into his box, and that if he wanted to know who'd left the message, he'd have to call the number. When he did, he reached an answering machine that delivered the following message: "Hi, this is Randy, please leave your name and leave your number. . . ."

I, too, have been the recipient of one of Randy's messages, delivered through Maria. In this case it came from someone I'd never even thought might have been in contact with me. I wore my great-aunt Rose's wedding ring for twenty-five years. It had never been off my finger since the day she gave it to me so that she could, as she put it, have the pleasure of seeing me wear it. Then, one day, I stopped by to visit with Maria, who told me that my aunt Rose had sent a message through Randy to be delivered to me. "Randy told me to tell you your aunt Rose says hello and that she's moving to a higher level," she said. I confess that I'd never been conscious of my aunt's presence. After receiving that message, however, I realized she must have been there all along. That's why she was letting me know she was now moving on in spirit.

Later that same evening, as if to confirm my newfound understanding, I felt something pinching my finger. When I looked to see what it might be, I discovered that Aunt Rose's ring, which I'd been wearing for a quarter of a century, had split completely in half. In that moment I was astounded. While it made sense to me that the release of my aunt's energy as she moved to a higher level had caused her ring to split, I was still dumbstruck. Rings split, certainly, especially rings as old as that one. But that hers would do so on the very day I received Randy's message was to me a dramatic manifestation of her spirit. To this day, every time I tell that story, I'm amazed. My great-aunt certainly took the meaning of coincidence to an entirely new spiritual level.

Maria also writes to Randy. One of those letters she showed me was particularly interesting because it validated so many of the ways I'd been aware of my mother's spirit manifesting itself to me. The letter was dated September 14, 1983, and the first few lines read:

> I am in NY and I think of you often. You have been coming through music a lot, I turn on the radio and there you are, confirming thoughts and messages that I have received from you. Sometimes when I receive messages from you I think it is my mind. I think that I am making it up and then comes a song [about] exactly what it was I was speaking of.

Maria and I haven't discussed the various songs she heard or what specific meaning they had for her. Yet the very fact that a song heard on the radio has, on more than one occasion, confirmed a message from her son immediately reminded me of the many times I've heard "La Vie en Rose" at a time and in a place that I absolutely *knew* to be a confirmation of my mother's presence.

Having seen for myself the kinds of information Randy was providing for Maria, I felt compelled to find out if I, too, could use this as a way of tapping into my psychic energy in order to connect with my mother. I was excited and incredibly curious to know whether I'd receive a response. I began by writing some basic questions to see what kinds of answers I'd receive. As I started to write, I could feel the energy in my body change. Although I was totally conscious, the words were flowing faster than I could think them. It wasn't until the writing stopped and I read what was on the paper that I actually knew what I'd written.

What has come through my pen over the years since I wrote

that first letter has been consistently astonishing to me. After my first attempt I began to keep a separate journal for specific questions. Now, I very often sit down quietly with a pad and pen, practice emptying my conscious mind, and simply let the writing come.

As I've said, each year since my mother died, on her birthday I've gotten a cold or the flu. In the third year after her death, I came down with a really bad case of the flu that seemed to last forever and that caused my left ear to clog so badly that I could hardly hear. When we're sick, our defenses are down, we're down, and we sometimes need someone to commiserate with us. In my misery I was really missing my mother, and I was wondering what she was up to and whom she was with. So I took out my journal and wrote the following simple questions: "Who are you with on the other side? Any family?" When I'd stopped writing, I found not only the answer to my question, but much more. First she said, "We're all here. I don't see them all the time, but it was great to be greeted by them and reconnect." Then she wrote that Grandma Dora, my father's mother, was there, still baking cakes and pies. And she mentioned someone called Jessica, a name I'd never even heard. When I phoned my father in Florida to ask if he knew who she was, he said that the name sounded familiar and suggested I check with my aunt. She, in turn, told me she knew there was a Jessica somehow related to her grandparents— my great-grandparents—but she wasn't sure exactly what the relationship had been.

One criterion used by psychic investigators—those who seek to confirm or disprove the validity of after-death communication through objective means—to determine whether or not a specific message is genuine is whether or not the recipient could have acquired the information through any other means. For me, finding the name Jessica in my journal was absolute confirmation that the information coming through my pen was being provided by my mother in spirit. What she went on to say in that same message, however, was not only even more validating but also enlightening to me. Here's what I found I had written:

> Fret not about your ear. It will clear up by Tuesday, no sooner. Because you're tuning in on a higher frequency, recognizing when and how to connect, in order to do the work on this next level, and your ear is the physical manifestation of adjusting to listen in.

Believe me, those were not thoughts I'd ever had about why my ear was so clogged. Clinically, I believe that physical symptoms may often be manifestations of grief or other psychological issues. In this instance I assumed that my lingering emotional pain, set off by my mother's birthday, had triggered my ear problem. I had never for a moment considered or recognized that my physical problem might be an extension of my spiritual journey. Her message helped to sustain me emotionally because it allowed me to understand how purposeful my ear pain really was. As a result, I was better able to tolerate the discomfort, feeling hopeful rather than anxious that it would persist indefinitely. My ear, by the way, did clear up exactly when my mother said it would.

Also, in the very same message, she acknowledged that she hadn't paid me a dream visit in a while by apologizing and saying, "Sorry I haven't visited recently in dreams. I've been quite busy flitting about. How do you like that word? Yes!"

Frankly, "flitting" is not a word that's ever been part of my vocabulary. It's not one I'd ever have thought of using. But there it was on the page. Imagine my wonder when, just a few days later, my patient Liza showed up in my office saying, "I saw this and thought of you." She had brought me a gift—a large pink fabric butterfly ornament with golden gossamer wings wearing a little name tag around it's neck that said . . . "Flitter!" I told her how touched I was by her thoughtful present and then shared with her how truly amazing her gift really was. To me it was yet another confirmation that my mother's spirit had come through in that written message. I still have that "Flitter" butterfly in my office, and whenever I look at it, I'm reminded of my mother's ongoing presence in my life.

So, while I know I will no longer receive cards and letters from my mother in my mailbox, I have the consolation of her messages from the spirit realm, preserved in my connection catalog, to add to those I received while she was alive.

Tapping into the Energy Source

In her seminal bestselling book, *The Artist's Way: A Spiritual Path to Higher Creativity,* Julia Cameron "links creativity to spirituality by showing how to connect with the creative energies of the universe." "What we are talking about," she says, "is an induced—or invited—spiritual experience. . . . If you think of the universe as a vast electrical sea in which you are immersed and from which you are formed, opening to your creativity changes you from something bobbing in that sea to a more fully functioning, more conscious, more cooperative part of the ecosystem."

Ms. Cameron is talking specifically to writers and artists about unleashing the powers of the unconscious mind from the constraints of so-called rational blocking mechanisms. Tapping into this kind of unconscious spiritual energy is not, however, limited to artists or writers. In fact, I think of the pen (or pencil, if you prefer) as a kind of plug that allows us all to connect with that universal source of spiritual energy.

While dream visits, manifestations, feeling a presence, or receiving the help we've asked for all serve to reinforce a sense that our loved ones are still with us, these modes of contact can also be extremely abstract, and we might sometimes need, or wish we could have, a more literal kind of communication. I know that one of the things I've missed most since my mother's death are the many notes, cards, and letters I received from her throughout my life, virtually all of which I still have in my possession. No longer receiving them left me with a profound feeling of emptiness, but because Maria had laid the groundwork for my understanding of the power of written communication, I was able to continue our loving correspondence in a new way.

Asking for Answers

If there are any questions you wish you could ask your loved one in spirit, why not do what I did? Use your pen as a way of connecting to the energy of the afterlife and see what kinds of answers you receive. You might simply be curious, as I was, to know whether or not your loved one will write back. There are however, other, more specifically therapeutic ways you can use channeled writing as a path to healing.

Because of my special bond with my mother, there was no unfinished business to settle when she died. We'd certainly said everything there was to say to one another about our feelings before she passed. I knew that she was aware of how much I loved her and how much I would miss her when she was gone. Sadly, however, many people don't have the opportunity to say what's in their hearts, or are caught up in unresolved conflicts that may be interfering with their ability to share loving feelings.

As has already been demonstrated in some of the stories I've told about friends and patients, the death of a loved one can leave the survivor wishing for another chance to close a rift, get answers to questions left unasked, or simply let his or her feelings be known. Writing from the heart can be one of the tools at our disposal for healing those rifts, getting answers to those questions, and resolving our feelings of guilt or anger, even after death. It is a powerful vehicle for sorting through the inner turmoil that can create rough seas in the wake of your loss.

If it's the answer to a question you need, I believe you can receive it in writing. If, before you start, you need to clear your mind of the censors or little Doubting Thomases that live up there in your rational consciousness, do the "Sign Language" meditation on pages 138–140. Have your pad and pencil with you, write a specific question, and just let the words flow. Ask whatever you like and keep on writing. Don't think it through. Don't worry about how you're expressing yourself. Grammar and punctuation are not important here. Let your writing arrive at its own conclusion and see what you find on the page.

If your questions are something like, "Why did you make it so difficult for me to become my own person?" or "Why could I never feel that you were really proud of me," or "Were you pleased with the way I turned out, and, if so, why didn't you ever tell me that?" you may be surprised by the answers you receive.

Are those answers really coming from your loved one in spirit? Personally, I believe they are. Clinically, I also know that, wherever they may originate, they can enable you to get past the self-censorship, self-doubt, disappointment, self-pity, and recriminations that can block the flow of your psychic energy.

So, whether the messages you are getting come from the spirit world or from within, they become testimony to your ability to harness your own subconscious spiritual energy. The answers you receive will strengthen your ability to trust in yourself and the decisions you make. As a result, you'll have taken an important healing step toward resolving issues and problems that may have been preventing you from moving forward with your life.

Writing from the heart is, for me, a kind of spontaneous communication, one that bypasses conscious thought and originates directly from our deepest, uncensored core—the place where our innate ability to connect with the world of spirit resides.

Let Your Feelings Flow

Writing, in this electronic and digital age, is becoming something of a lost art. Which is too bad, for many reasons. How many of us ever go to the mailbox these days and find a long letter from a friend? From the time I went away to school almost to the time she died, I received and cherished witty, informative, and loving notes from my mother. I don't think any e-mail can ever replace the handwritten, personal warmth of a tactile, savable letter, to be reread and refolded over time. Now that she's gone, I'm more grateful than ever that I've held on to her writings, because they continue to amuse and delight me time after time. Whenever I read one, it in some way brings her back to life, if only for a moment.

And do young girls still pour out their hearts and secret feelings to a diary kept locked and hidden in a drawer? In years gone by, writers, men of letters, and thinkers of audacious thoughts kept diaries that have become records of their lives and a legacy for succeeding generations. Keeping a journal not only provided one with a written record of daily life, it also allowed proper ladies an outlet for deeply secret improper thoughts and gentlemen an outlet for venting feelings they couldn't express out loud. These were, in effect, therapeutic tools that allowed for a kind of self-analysis and purging of unexpressed emotions. Writing a letter to a loved one in spirit can, I believe, serve that same constructive therapeutic purpose.

Some of us don't mind voicing our thoughts and feelings aloud, even to one who is no longer physically present. But for others, that might seem too much like talking to oneself—just a little bit too awkward for comfort. Some of us are not so adept at verbalizing our thoughts and feelings. If you're able to speak to your loved one out loud, without censoring yourself, by all means do so. I believe he or she will hear you. If, however, you feel more comfortable or safer with the silence of the written word, I would urge you to try writing a letter to the spirit realm. It's an incredibly effective way to promote emotional growth and facilitate the corrective healing that's necessary in the aftermath of a conflicted, negative, or unresolved relationship.

Here are a few guidelines I suggest my patients follow when they are writing from the heart:

- *Just let the words flow.* The point of your writing is to side-step your conscious mind so that it doesn't censor your thoughts and feelings. Just as when you're asking for answers, try to send your conscious mind off on a little vacation so that your unconscious psychic energy can roam free.
- *Be direct.* If you had trouble speaking your mind or from your heart when your loved one was alive, now's the time to do it. That's why you're writing this letter, and no one but the person you're addressing ever needs to know about it.

- *Let go of your secrets.* If you've been harboring some secret hurt or shame—something your loved one did to you, perhaps inadvertently, or you did to him or her and never confessed—this is when you need to let it out. Get rid of the burden by sharing it in a safe environment free from fear or punishment.

- *Avoid finger-pointing.* If you have been blaming the person you're writing to for something you think he or she did to you, and you're only engaging in this exercise to rehash hard feelings, you'll just be reinforcing and justifying those emotions instead of freeing yourself from them.

- *Forgiveness need not be a foregone conclusion.* If you begin this process assuming that you *have to* forgive your loved one for something; if you believe that you *must* express only loving and compassionate thoughts and feelings, you'll be censoring yourself before you begin, and you might just finish by feeling even angrier or more hurt than when you started. Remember that this is like writing in a diary; it's for letting out real emotions and reaching out beyond the grave. You can reach out in love and forgiveness certainly, but you can also reach out in anger, frustration, or need. They are all equally valid feelings so long as they are real.

In *Writing Down the Bones: Freeing the Writer Within,* Natalie Goldberg teaches would-be writers

> to burn through to first thoughts, to the place where energy is unobstructed by social politeness or the internal censor, to the place where you are writing what your mind actually sees and feels, not what it *thinks* it should see or feel.

That is also the purpose of this kind of letter writing, as it is the purpose of all transcommunication.

Whether we're asking for a sign, communicating in the world of dreams, or writing to the spirit realm, what we're tapping into is a source spiritual energy that is beyond conscious thought. Whether we get there through meditation, hypnosis, or simply letting our subconscious out of the mental basement where the ego usually keeps it caged, the important thing is to give ourselves permission to roam beyond rational thought and engage with the stream of energy that lies beyond the bounds of time and space.

Sometimes when I discuss the power of writing with a patient, I'm aware that he or she is harboring a particular grievance or constellation of grievances whose resolution requires a more structured kind of communication than the simple pouring out of uncensored emotions. While sometimes the process of venting bottled-up emotion is all that's required for release, at other times we need to feel that our loved one is hearing and responding to us as he or she never did in life. If you are one of these people, I suggest you do the following exercise, which I call "Eternal Dialogue." It's a way to help you identify those areas where you may be holding onto your grief so that you can work through unresolved conflicts and release the negative emotions you've been carrying around—emotions that may be weighing you down and preventing you from moving forward.

1. Make a list of the three main grievances you hold against your departed loved one. For example: "You didn't support me." "You never listened." "You were always so control-

ling." "You abused me physically and emotionally when you drank too much." "You always blamed me for everything."

2. Now, identify the feelings each of these grievances evoked in you. For example: unloved; angry and resentful; scared; nervous or anxious; insecure; worthless; ridiculed; deprived; ignored; cheated; abandoned; helpless; bad; lazy; powerless; stupid or ignorant.

3. Go back to the memory of the experiences that evoked these emotions and write your loved one how you felt: "When you blamed me, I felt stupid." "When you didn't listen, I felt ignored." "When you abused me, I felt helpless."

4. Articulate what you believe to be the reasons for your loved one's behavior. For example, "I think you blamed me all the time because Mom blamed you so much." Or, "I think you abused me because you drank to push away the pain of your own childhood."

5. Now express what you wished for and how you'd have liked him or her to respond. **Wish:** I wish you'd supported me so that I'd felt you loved me. **Response:** I'm sorry I always blamed you. **Wish:** I wish you'd appreciated my efforts so that I didn't feel so worthless. **Response:** I'm sorry I made you feel worthless.

6. Forgive and release both yourself and your loved one from past behaviors. For example, you might write, "I'm sorry if I wasn't the daughter (son, partner, wife, husband, etc.) you wanted. Let's find a new way to connect."

7. Request a change in your relationship. For example, "I'd like to feel your support in my life."

This kind of letter to the spirit realm differs from channeled writing in that the writer is not actually expecting to receive answers from the world of spirit. Rather, the answers we receive come from within. It is, nevertheless, a powerful tool for reconnecting with the departed. Through writing you can reconstruct your relationships in ways that allow you to redress unresolved grievances. You can also release those unexpressed or buried emotions that may be preventing you from regaining your emotional balance.

Many people are carrying anger, hurt, and pain inside them simply because they believe they have no other recourse since their loved one is now gone. Or, as my patient Melissa put it to me not so long ago, with reference to the unresolved resentments she was dealing with following the death of her father, "How could I be mad at someone who was ill?"

Melissa had originally come to me because of problems she was having both at work and in her current relationship. It was in the course of our discussing these problems that her unresolved conflicts with her father began to surface.

The man she was then seeing was both negative and blaming and had a way of spoiling Melissa's enjoyment, even if it involved something as innocuous as her wanting to order dessert in a restaurant. Inevitably, her decision would escalate into a control issue that ultimately made her feel guilty and left a bad taste in her mouth.

In addition to being unhappy in her relationship, Melissa was not satisfied in her work. She's an extremely successful lawyer but doesn't really love what she's doing. What she's always wanted to be is a writer, but she's never felt fully free to pursue her passion as a career choice.

Once Melissa came to realize, in the course of our sessions, that her current relationship was replicating the relationship she'd had with her father, she was able finally to end it and move on. Perhaps even more important, however, was her realization that working in a profession she'd never aspired to was also an extension of her father's influence.

Her father, she told me, was extremely controlling and critical, and one of the ways he exerted control was by being unreasonably cheap. He would pay for her college education only if she enrolled in the program he determined she should follow. In fact, while she was growing up, he refused to pay for *anything* he deemed unimportant, which might include a necessary haircut or new clothes for school. Not only writing but also reading were way up at the top of unimportant pastimes. After a while he'd so tarnished her pleasure that she even gave up reading for a time. She'd always been resentful of his controlling behavior, but when he became ill she stopped—or thought she'd stopped—being angry with him. Except that we can't just will ourselves to stop being angry. What we do instead is to bottle up or suppress those emotions, which then manifest themselves in other ways. In Melissa's case, because she felt she could no longer be angry with her father, she found another man whose controlling personality was similar to her father's and continued experiencing conflict with him.

I explained to Melissa that only by expressing her true feelings of anger and disappointment would she be able to move past the guilt that was keeping her stuck and release the creative energy she'd been keeping bottled inside. I suggested that she try the writing exercise I've just described above. These are a few of the grievances she put on paper, exactly as she wrote them:

- The way I'd hear those voices in my head for years and years, telling me not to do it that way and not to do some other thing. Endless scrutiny that made me want to explode.
- Constantly justifying the refusal to spend money.
- Endlessly being told that I was always *reading,* and finally giving it up for years.

Then, for the second part of the exercise, Melissa wrote some of the answers she wished she could have heard while her father was alive.

- I'm really proud of you. I'm lucky to have you as a daughter.
- I think you're talented and smart and special.
- I should have been more supportive of the decisions you made. I should have allowed others to have ideas instead of supporting only whatever ideas I came up with, and dismissing the rest as bad or ridiculous.

In clinical terms, Melissa was experiencing the power of the superego, which is the internalized code of authority, typically that of a parent. All of us hear that inner voice from our childhood that provides us with our moral code and guides us in our behavior, helping us to determine right from wrong and good from bad. When we listen to the voice of our superego, it often echoes the critical or negative tone we heard from our parent. The potency of the "Eternal Dialogue" exercise is that it softens the harshness of your superego's critical voice. It does this by helping you to develop compassion for yourself so that you become able to validate yourself even though your parents did not. By doing that, you can learn to give yourself the approval and acknowledgment that will enhance your self-esteem. Melissa had always known that she'd be writing one day; she just didn't know when that day would come. She is now actively pursuing her writing career and has almost completed her first novel.

Reclaiming Your Self

The grievances you hold against someone who's died may, without your having consciously realized it, have affected your thoughts and feelings not only about the person whom you believe to have hurt you but also about yourself. If you know that another person's actions or behavior caused you to *feel* stupid or unloved or worthless, you may have come to believe that you *are* actually stupid or unlovable or worthless. If that's the case, and your loved one is no longer available to tell you it isn't so, you may feel robbed of the opportunity to heal those wounds. If that's the case, writing provides yet another opportunity for you to do the work you may have needed or wanted to do on yourself while that person was alive. Rather than addressing conflicts you may have had with the departed, you can focus on your own vulnerabilities. Through writing, you can turn your fearful, futile, or negative thoughts and emotions into affirmations of healing and self-worth.

The efficacy of this kind of writing, like that of hypnosis, lies in the power words have to affect our thoughts. In other words, when you think positively on the unconscious level, those thoughts will be manifested in positive behavior. The unconscious is extremely literal and records the words you use, which is why it's so important to articulate your thoughts in the positive and to change the tone of the critical voice in our head. If you're to gain the full effect of the affirmation, it's important that you state things to yourself in the positive. You need, for example, to say, "I'm feeling more secure and confident," rather than stating it in the negative as, "I'm not going to be insecure anymore." The former is giving yourself something positive *to do* while the latter would be continuing to criticize yourself.

The power of positive thinking is not a myth. When Dr. Norman Vincent Peale said, "Change your thoughts and you change your world," he was talking about the power of that interplay of thought and behavior that can change the trajectory of our lives. The following exercise, which I've named "Accentuate the Positive," can help you to transform critical thoughts into positive ones and to translate "af*fear*mations" into affirmations so that you can "firm up" your self-esteem and, by changing your thoughts, change your behavior.

- Go back to "Eternal Dialogue" on pages 190–191 and look at the negative feelings you wrote down in Step 2.
- List those feelings down the left side of your page:

> Unloved
> Angry and resentful
> Scared, nervous, and anxious
> Insecure
> Worthless
> Ridiculed
> Deprived or cheated
> Ignored
> Abandoned
> Helpless

Bad

Lazy

Powerless

Stupid and ignorant

- Now, on the right side of the page, write an affirmation that negates that emotion.

Unloved	I am lovable.
Angry and resentful	I am accepting and tolerant.
Scared, nervous, and anxious	I feel calm and in control.
Insecure	I feel secure within myself.
Worthless	I am a worthwhile human being who is fortunate to have so many talents and abilities.
Ridiculed	I feel confident in myself.
Deprived or cheated	I feel complete with what I have. I feel like a whole person.
Ignored	I feel noticed and special.
Abandoned	I am grounded in my life and able to take care of myself.
Helpless	I feel strong and able to protect myself.
Bad	I am a good and loving person.

Lazy	I feel motivated to accomplish my goals, energized to face the day.
Powerless	I feel empowered on a daily basis.
Stupid and ignorant	I am intelligent, aware, and knowledgeable.

- Once you've chosen the affirmation or affirmations appropriate to your own feelings and circumstances, make a point of writing it (or them) down or saying them aloud to yourself each morning and evening until they've become your own. You'll be surprised and gratified to discover how completely you can transform negative emotions into positive ones simply by reframing them and confirming them through the power of positive thought and the written word.

The Positive Energy of Writing from the Heart

When it comes to healing from loss, the pen is definitely mightier than the sword. If we're carrying around negative thoughts and emotions about a loved one who's died, those thoughts and emotions will become like concealed weapons that we use unconsciously to continue the emotional battle. It then becomes impossible for us to make peace either with the deceased or with ourselves. As a result, we'll be unable to complete the grieving process in a way that allows us to create positive changes for ourselves.

If we put down the sword and take up the pen, we can use writing from the heart as a way to continue contact with our loved one in spirit as well as to make deeper and more meaningful contact with ourselves so that we can achieve more peace, comfort, and growth. As my patient Melissa said to me in a recent session, "It's amazing how much freer I feel. I'm so much less angry than I've been in a long time."

7.

Recovery and Renewal of Afterlife Relationships

The bitterest tears shed over graves are for words left unsaid and deeds left undone.

—HARRIET BEECHER STOWE

Writing is one method at your disposal for continuing to engage with those in spirit. As you've seen, it can be especially helpful when you need to heal the hurt, release pent-up anger or guilt, and resolve the negative emotions that may have been holding you back. It is far from the only tool at your disposal. All the other forms of transcommunication can also be profoundly healing. They can help you to gain a new understanding of old wounds, achieve mutual forgiveness with those who have departed, and improve relationships with the living. Transcommunication can even help you to initiate a dialogue with those in spirit where none existed in life.

Any kind of negative emotional energy, whatever its source,

can keep you stuck in relationships or situations that are unful-filling. How this happens was demonstrated in the story of my patient Anne Marie, whose relationship with her father was, with-out her realizing it, playing a significant role in keeping her locked in an apartment she'd long since outgrown. Anne Marie's father had always been there for her when he was alive, so when he died a part of her died as well. Without his support, she felt alone in the world, and it was often difficult for her to manage on her own. When she reconnected with him through transcommuni-cation, she realized that he could still be there to provide his support when she needed it. That understanding has enabled her to finally move forward and feel freer than ever before in the years since his death.

Anne Marie, as it happens, had a warm and loving relation-ship with her father. Without realizing it, she was holding on to him by remaining stuck in that apartment. If, however, your re-lationship with someone in spirit was less than warm and loving, the residue of negative energy also continue to limit you. By find-ing a way to release it, you will be releasing yourself from its stifling bond.

Ariel is a rabbi and the daughter of a rabbi. Because she grew up with spirituality permeating her home, she has always been open to the possibility of communicating with a world beyond the physical. But she was also the fourth of five children and her father, despite his religious calling, had been cold and unloving to her. To demonstrate his lack of caring, she told me about the time when, filling out an application for life insurance and asked to list the names and ages of the children, he forgot to include hers.

Although she felt called to follow in his spiritual footsteps, she understood that she would first have to resolve the negative emotions she was carrying with regard to his fathering. Her familiarity with prayer and communicating with the world of spirit had already opened her to the concept of transcommunication. She was, therefore, willing to "speak" to her father and express her feelings of having been unloved and less special than her siblings. In fact, she felt able to be open and honest with him for the first time in her life. After allowing herself to express her negative feelings, she was able to acknowledge the good in him that, because of her anger, she couldn't acknowledge when he was alive. She was then able to appreciate that he gave her a love of knowledge, a delight in ideas, and a strong commitment to serving others. Through her new understanding, she experienced loving feelings toward her father that enabled her to genuinely connect and bond with him.

She now wears one of her father's prayer shawls, given to her by her mother when she was ordained. Every Saturday morning before she begins the service, she turns her back to her congregation and has a moment of private communion with him. She holds the prayer shawl over her head before placing it around her shoulders and invites him to join her for the next two hours. Ariel believes now that he's there to protect her, and she feels that he's very present in her life at that moment.

According to Jewish practice, one is supposed to kiss the prayer shawl before putting it on, but because Ariel wears lipstick, she touches it to her cheek instead. When she does that, she feels as if her father is kissing her on the cheek and giving her his blessing.

Letting Go of Bottled-up Anger

One of the most remarkable stories of healing I've ever heard was told to me by Laura, a massage therapist and yoga teacher and the director of the meditation group at the Metaphysical Center of New Jersey. She is a woman of extraordinary energy and deep spirituality. Laura had been estranged from and angry with her father for many years. He'd walked out on his family when she was nine years old, and as a result she grew up feeling abandoned and neglected by him.

Sometime ago, she told me that for about a year, whenever she drove down the street, the streetlights would go out around her. Once, when she was at a football stadium, four rows of six lights each went out over where she was sitting; the other lights remained on. Because of my own experiences, I was aware that such powerful electronic disturbances often signal the presence of spiritual energy. I therefore asked Laura who she thought was trying to contact her. She, however, was very skeptical. Despite her long experience with guided meditation, she'd never considered the possibility of direct conscious contact. Her interpretation of the phenomenon had been that she was being to drained of physical energy by the massage work she was doing and was actually replenishing her energy from the lights. "It was a reflection of my own energy level, not energy that was coming from the spiritual realm." I suggested that she reconsider, and so she did a meditation during which she connected with a spirit guide. That connection triggered for her the realization that if she could connect with an anonymous or unknown person in spirit, she could also connect with someone she'd known in life. Following that insight, the lights stopped going out for a time. As a result, Laura began to consider that her experience had been in some way spiritually generated.

When, several months later, the lights started to go out again, she was more open to their spiritual significance. She was leading a client in meditation one day when the client said that her spirit guide was named Sarah, which was the name of Laura's grand-mother. The mention of that name triggered for Laura the memory of a psychic's having told her, several years before, "Your grandmother Sarah has a message for you." "But," Laura told me, "I was much younger then, I hadn't had much of a relationship with my grandmother when she died, and the message didn't really mean anything to me, so I forgot about it." Now she asked the client's spirit guide, "Are you my grandmother?" and the client answered, "No, but she's here." Because this was a client, Laura didn't press her further at the time.

Afterwards, however, she went to the sanctuary where she did her meditations and asked her spirit guide if her grandmother had a message for her. "Yes," came the answer. "Contact her in a meditation." In her meditation Laura saw her father as a much younger man curled in a fetal position and heard the voice of her grandmother saying, "He was neglected; he didn't get the love he needed as a child." The voice went on to say that he was the second youngest of ten siblings who had tried to toughen him up by bullying him, that he'd felt very alone, much smaller and weaker, and that he'd grown up feeling intimidated and fearful.

Laura then visualized healing her father by surrounding him with white light, and she tried to understand and forgive him. The next day, while doing her yoga, she felt a great release in her side, which was where she believed she held her anger. "I realized that I was no longer angry with my father, that all my anger with him had diminished." Since then she's been able to accept him for who he is, has been able to reconnect, and can call and speak to him when she wants to.

At that point Laura told me that her grandmother, in her meditation, had also given her a message for her father, which was, "She sends you light and love and is sorry for neglecting you, and it's okay to have compassion for yourself. It's time to stand up and not be afraid to move forward. She loves you and your brothers. Forgive, let it go, leave it behind. You are powerful and highly intelligent. Let go of the illusion that you are not."

Naturally enough, I asked if she'd delivered the message, and she told me she hadn't—she'd forgotten. Laura's grandmother had certainly helped her to understand the reasons underlying her father's behavior and to begin healing her relationship with him. It was clear to me, however, that she hadn't yet let go of her anger completely enough to help him out by delivering the message.

Sometime later she told me that, after our conversation, she'd been thinking about why she'd forgotten to deliver her grandmother's message. She realized that she'd recently been angry with her father and that they hadn't spoken in several months. "He was upset that I'd forgotten his birthday, and I was angry with him for not understanding that we don't have a great relationship to start out, that I'm very busy, and that we shouldn't stand on formalities." So she called him up and asked him to come over and join her in a meditation.

Before taking him into the meditation, she told him that his mother had given her a message for him, and he seemed comfortable with that. When his spirit guide appeared, she read her father the message and then said, "Okay, now call your mother in." His mother appeared and told him, "Go to my grave and let it all out." Laura interpreted "it" to mean all the pain and hurt he'd been holding onto. She asked him to hold his mother's hand, but he refused, so the spirit guide took Laura's father's hand and his mother's in each of his own to connect them. His mother sent

Laura's father her love through the guide. As Laura said, "This was a healing experience for both me and my father. Now I can begin to reconnect with him."

She received further validation when, the following night, as she was walking through the streets, the lights began to go off. Fully tuned in by this time, she realized that someone must have been trying to get through to her, so the next day she returned to the meditation sanctuary. She immediately saw her grandmother's face and heard the words, "You did it. Thank you."

Laura told me that her father had not yet gone to his mother's grave, but she said, "The seed has been planted." Meanwhile, her grandmother in spirit has brought about a healing reconnection between her son and his daughter. Whether Laura's father will be able to transform his own relationship with his mother will be up to him. She has made it known that she's there to help and support him if he's willing to reach out.

Sometimes all that's necessary to rid ourselves of anger is to understand that even though our loved one may have hurt us, he or she was doing the best he could within his own limitations. Even if we were too emotionally injured or shut down in anger to come to that realization while he or she was alive, we can still, through transcommunication, renew and revitalize our relationship in the afterlife. Angie, whose astonishing communications with her brother-in-law Eric we've already discussed, had just such a healing experience when she learned that the grandfather she'd been angry with since childhood had made it clear he was reaching out from the world of spirit in order to make amends.

Angie told me what upset her most when her grandfather died. "I was left alone with all these bad feelings that I no longer had a chance to resolve." She was hurt, she said, because he'd always wrongfully blamed her for so many things. One incident she never forgot occurred when she was nine or ten years old. She had been standing outside the house talking with him when, inside, two of her sisters knocked over a shelf and broke a piece of bric-a-brac. Her grandfather immediately phoned her father and told him that Angie had done it, which he obviously knew wasn't true, since she'd been with him when it happened. She'd never understood why he did those sorts of things and had been too intimidated and scared to ask him. Their legacy left her feeling unloved, worthless, and cast in the role of the black sheep of the family.

After his death she never really dealt with all these feelings but more or less put them out of her mind. Thirty years later a psychic told her, "Your grandfather walks with you," and then spoke the name Joseph, so Angie knew it was really him. "He's always there," the psychic said. "He's holding out yellow roses." Initially his presence frightened Angie, and all her buried feelings toward him began to resurface. Gradually, however, she became more open to the possibility of talking to him and trying to heal. Just knowing she could do that gave her a sense of peace. She began to ask, "Why did you treat me that way?" and thoughts would come into her mind. She heard his voice saying he'd wanted her to be perfect, had wanted her to behave a certain way. "It wasn't about me," she said. "It was about his own expectations coupled with his limitations, not mine. He couldn't be there for me as a kid because he couldn't deal with me, but perhaps he could be there for me now. I was able to come to terms with that and be at peace."

Angie was able to realize that even though her grandfather may have hurt her, he was doing the best he could. Moreover, through transcommunication she realized he was trying to heal the wounds he was aware of having caused. While that knowledge couldn't change the past, it did enable her to release all the pent-up anger she had carried through the years. As an outgrowth of that, she was finally able to find something positive in a relationship that had for so long been both inexplicable and negative for her.

Sara, who had reached out to heal old wounds with her father before his death, nevertheless discovered that all her anger had not yet been resolved. Although she's generally a happy person, sometimes her anger and resentment still creep up and take her unaware. On this particular occasion she was in northern California during the winter following her father's death. It was cold. She was all alone, and she was feeling sad and sorry for herself. In the midst of her melancholy, she began talking out loud to him, blaming him for all the abuses she believed he'd inflicted on her as a child. "It's all your fault," she told him. "It's because of you that I'm feeling unhappy." All of a sudden the electricity went off, leaving her without heat or light. "I knew it was my father," she told me, "acknowledging that he had heard me. I'd never been able to express these feelings when he was alive, because I'd always been too frightened of him. It was so healing to know that I could be open with him now, and that he was responding."

Most often the emotional wounds we suffer in life are not intentionally inflicted. There are people, however, who have themselves sustained so much emotional damage as children that their behavior as adults does seem to be deliberately malicious or evil.

While I was writing this book, I was put in touch with many people who had compelling experiences to relate. One of the most dramatic of these stories was told to me by Dolores and her mother, who had each been paid the very same dream visit by Dolores's grandmother, her mother's mother.

Dolores was with her mother one day about four or five years after her grandmother's death when she mentioned that she'd had an amazing dream. In it, she said her grandmother was "on her knees" and crying. Dolores told her mother that, in the dream, she'd gone over to her grandmother and embraced her. It was at that point that Dolores's mother said she too had had a dream in which her mother was crying. "What did you do when you saw your mother crying like that?" Dolores asked. "Were you able to comfort her?" And her mother replied, "No, I stood there and looked and looked at her."

What makes the experience so powerful, in addition to their both having had the same dream, is that, as Dolores told it to me, she'd "never *ever* seen Nana cry." In fact, she said that when she was a little girl of maybe five or six, she'd actually fantasized about killing her grandmother because of all the evil things her mother had told her about the way she'd been treated as a child. Dolores's grandmother was an abusive mother who'd done terrible things to her children. She'd beaten Dolores's mother black-and-blue and then kept her home from school until she was "presentable" enough to return. She and her husband went off for weeks at a time, leaving the children alone with all the food locked away except for the flour and water.

"She was devious and sick," Dolores said, "so it took a lot for me to find a way to love her. Over time I managed to do that, but I knew I could never trust her." As she grew up, Dolores came to understand that her grandmother had experienced her own traumatic childhood, which had contributed to making her the angry, hurtful woman she'd become. "Because it's family," she said, "you find a way to love that person while still watching your back. I felt there had to be some good in my grandmother, but it was hard to find it in life."

Fifteen years after she had that dream, Dolores went to a psychic, who told her, "Your mother's mother is trying to help out." When Dolores expressed her disbelief, the psychic said, "Sometimes people do make a turnaround on the other side. She's trying very hard to help out; she's trying very hard." So the dreams Dolores and her mother had so many years before helped her to believe that "maybe she had changed, maybe *now* something positive could happen." Even though her grandmother had not, in so many words, expressed her regret, the psychic had validated Dolores's dream.

For Dolores's mother it was a different story. In order to survive she'd run away from home at the age of sixteen. Despite all that had happened, however, she still tried to communicate with and reach out to her mother until the last ten years of her life. Then, out of a need to protect herself, she pulled away entirely. When her mother was dying, she went back out of a sense of duty to see her through her last days. That was okay for her, she said. "But I don't have feelings of love for her. I couldn't change the way I felt after all the things she'd done to me in her life. The dream made me think she's trying, and that's wonderful. I'm not afraid of her anymore. Maybe I just need to have a give-and-take with her."

Both women felt that their dreams were truly communications from the world of spirit. Dolores said, "I felt it was really happening, that for the first time my grandmother was really expressing sadness through her tears. When Mom had the same dream, I was sure. I'd always felt something for her, and the dream was a kind of corroboration of what I felt."

Dolores was able to embrace more fully than her mother the belief that her grandmother might really have changed and might truly regret the damage she'd caused in her life. In fact, she said, somewhat ruefully, "I have a teacup of hers that I've kept, but I've never had a cup of tea in it. Now I think I might consider using it." Her mother, however, because she was damaged more deeply than Dolores, was not yet able to step forward and embrace her mother. She is, nevertheless, willing to acknowledge that in the dream she conveyed that she might actually have regrets about her actions. That understanding has softened her heart to the point where she is open to the possibility of there being a give-and-take between them. For Dolores, that dream visit validated her ability to empathize with the grandmother she'd initially hated so much and fantasized about killing. For her mother it brought the understanding that her mother was at last acknowledging and regretting the damage she'd done.

Emme, the plus-size supermodel whose dream helped her to deal with the death of her mother, has shared with me her own profound wisdom about making peace with those with whom you had a troubled relationship in life. "When you have a bad relationship with someone," she says, "it's almost as if you want to cleanse the palate and lean on those things you know were positive so that you don't attract any negativity around you, especially with someone who gave you a difficult time. You want to move on from being bound to that person by guilt or shame or anger. You don't want to let him or her bring you down anymore. You want to be able to make peace with their spirit so that you can release the baggage that tied you to them and can put it to rest."

Emme has written and spoken openly about her abusive relationship with her stepfather. When he died, she wanted to be

her death, Wilma said that her mother had been ill with rheumatic fever when she was three. At the age of sixty-six she had suffered a heart attack that, as it turned out, was caused by an aneurysm she'd developed as a result of the fever but had never known about. When she was in the hospital following the heart attack, she met a young doctor who told her about a new kind of procedure that was being done in Boston. As a result of that conversation, she became one of the first people ever to receive a balloon angioplasty. She lived ten more years, but because of the aneurysm, which could burst at any minute, Wilma explained, she was in effect a walking time bomb.

The eldest of four children, with three younger brothers, Wilma was, by her own admission, a real daddy's girl. Her father had never approved of the men she dated; they never seemed to quite measure up, and she believed that he had never really wanted her to get married. Because of that notion, she took a long time finding the right man. She was forty-seven years old when she finally announced her plans to marry the man she'd been dating for the past fifteen years. Her fear was that in some way the emotional separation would be so dramatic that it actually might kill her parents. Even though she was living three thousand miles away—she in San Francisco, they on the East Coast—and was financially independent, she was plagued by separation anxiety and the guilt that accompanied it. She also knew the announcement would throw her mother into overdrive, planning and orchestrating the wedding. She worried about her mother's health and the danger that she might further deplete her already limited energies. At the same time, however, her anxiety was balanced by her belief that her mother would be happy for her, and that she'd hang in there for the wedding.

Her mother did throw herself into preparing for the wedding, overseeing even the minutest details. So, when Wilma arrived home one Friday evening at nine o'clock, exhausted from a long day, she didn't answer the phone when it rang, thinking it was probably her mother calling to discuss some arrangement. When the machine picked up, she heard her mother's voice saying, "Wilma, are you there? Honey, if you're there, please pick up." And then, somewhat sadly, "Well, I guess you're not there. Just call me when you can." She was so tired that she figured she'd return the call in the morning, which, she said, meant to her, "I'll deal with Mom in the morning." She'd forgotten that she had an appointment in the morning and that she wouldn't be able to call before she left because of the time difference.

When she got home again at noon, there was a message from her brother asking her to call home. Heartbreakingly, he gave her the news that her mother had died that morning. Wilma was in shock. *Now I'll never get to return that phone call,* she thought. The guilt she felt at not having picked up her phone was totally devastating. "Why didn't I pick up that phone when my mother, the most important person in my life, needed to talk to me?" The last memory she'd have of her mother, she thought, was of not answering the phone, and she'd have to live with it the rest of her life. She described feeling as if she'd been run over by a car. What made her feel even worse was the realization that she couldn't even tell anyone in her family what had happened. Certainly not her brothers, who would only make her feel more guilty, if that were possible. "I felt," she said, "like I was the catalyst for a whole series of events I predicted when I picked up the phone to announce I was getting married, including the fear that it would kill my parents. On some level I now felt I'd been right. Indeed, it had killed my mother. No one in the family said to me 'you caused it,' but I felt I had."

She went back home for the funeral, and, while she was there, she went out to lunch with Dolores's mother. It was February, and they were sitting by the window in a restaurant overlooking an icy lake, talking about Wilma's mother. There was an empty third seat at the table on which they both put their pocket books. Wilma observed out loud that that would have been her mother's chair, and both women acknowledged that they felt her spirit was with them. Just then, they looked out the window and there, stuck in a tree, was a bunch of violet balloons. Virtually in unison they both said that it was Wilma's mother's presence. They didn't know why, but they both felt it.

At about that time her father was diagnosed as being in the early stages of Alzheimer's disease, and Wilma was concerned about him. One night she dreamt that he was in the kitchen. She was afraid he'd become confused, so she went in to find him and ran right into her mother. Her mom was wearing the gray dress she'd been buried in. She appeared to be "very hungry. She was making herself a snack, and was obviously very much alive." Wilma was about to say, "I thought you were dead," but didn't want her mother to know she'd thought that, so she stopped herself. Her mother then said, "I know, you thought I was dead, but I'm not." "I was so thrilled," Wilma told me. "She looked so beautiful, absolutely radiant. I said to her, 'Won't it be a great joke when everyone who was at the funeral finds out you're not dead.'" Then her mother said, "I have a big hole in my heart. It's all true." And that was the end of the dream.

"In that dream visit," Wilma told me, "I was celebrating that she was alive. If anyone had the power to contact me and the motivation to reach through the boundaries, it was my mother, because she could see how distraught I was over her death."

Several months later, in June, Wilma was back in California, at her cabin on the Russian River, when three purple balloons came floating out of nowhere into her yard. She knew it was her mother, and in her excitement she tried to grab them and bring them to safety, but they broke. She was quite astonished by the whole event because, she said, "There was no reason for *any* balloons to be blowing around the place, much less purple ones like those I'd seen by the lake."

This extraordinary series of contacts continued. Two days before the destruction of the World Trade Center, Wilma was in New England, staying at a house in the woods that had belonged to a friend whose estate she was settling as executor. She'd traveled with another friend who was making a documentary about Native Americans, and they'd gone to a reservation together on an information-gathering expedition. As her friend was leaving her for the night, Wilma said, "You know, I'm really a little afraid to stay here by myself. I feel as if the Indians are going to come out of the woods and attack me." After assuring her that she was being quite ridiculous and would be perfectly safe, her friend left. The next morning, at the edge of the woods, she found three violet balloons. This time, although she was surprised, she decided to leave them alone. "I felt it was a warning from my mother that something terrible would happen to my family." She didn't want to touch the balloons because she was afraid she'd break them. She felt that her mother's spirit was hovering around the house, and she wanted her to continue to be there. "Those balloons really comforted me," she said.

"My mother always paid attention to world events," Wilma told me. "And she always chided me for not doing so." The following day the Twin Towers fell, and Wilma later found out that one of the planes leaving Boston had followed a flight path that took it directly over the house where she was staying.

Those purple balloons were incredibly healing for Wilma. She recognized them as her mother's way of letting her know that she didn't have to feel guilty either about getting married or about not having answered the phone that fateful night. She shared with me, however, that she'd never really understood why her mother had chosen balloons as her way of connecting. Wilma believed it was because her mother had retained a sense of gleeful childishness throughout her life. I suggested to her that balloons were meant to signify that it was okay for her to release her guilt, since very often that's what we do with balloons. We set them free in the sky. I also reminded her that her mother had been one of the first patients to receive the balloon angioplasty that had saved her life, so balloons might very well have taken on a special significance for her.

"You know," Wilma said, "my mother was clinically dead at the time of her angioplasty and that balloon was her only contact with the earth."

"So," I continued, "she was still connecting with earth through balloons."

Wilma thanked me profusely for making that association and went on to say, "I didn't entirely get the meaning, and my mother would have expected me to get it right away."

At the time Wilma may have been too emotionally involved in her experiences to see the symbolic connections that were so apparent to me. More importantly, however, she certainly got the significance of her mother's reaching out to let her know that she didn't have to feel guilty. Because of that, she's been able to make peace with herself and with her mother's death. She's been able to move on with her own life. She did get married, and she's a successful working artist in San Francisco.

*   *   *

Sometimes guilt can be truly self-inflicted, even if, logically, we know that we did everything we could for our loved one. That is exactly what happened to Flo when her mother died. Flo had lived with her family in New York for thirty years, but when her father died, she decided to move to Virginia Beach. She told her mother about her plans to leave and said, "You can stay here, or you can come with me." "Where you go, I go," was her mother's immediate response.

As Flo told it to me, her mother was beginning to become senile, so, as soon as they arrived in Virginia Beach, she started to act as if she were on vacation. She denied that they actually lived there and was angry with her daughter for having, as she believed, forced her to move. She was driving Flo crazy by constantly asking when they were going home. No matter how many times Flo told her, "This is where we live now," she persisted.

It was hard for Flo to reconcile herself to her mother's anger. She felt hurt, particularly because there was substantial evidence that her mother was actually enjoying her time in Virginia Beach. Flo had enrolled her in a senior citizens group, where she played bridge on a regular basis. She'd be smiling when she left home and smiling as she got off the bus on her return, but the minute she saw Flo, her smile disappeared. There was even a picture of her with her bridge cronies in the local newspaper that showed her smiling broadly. But because she wanted her daughter to feel guilty, she could never let her know she was having a good time. "I just felt sad and sorry that she couldn't enjoy the house and the time we were spending together," Flo told me. "I was taking her everywhere with me, and yet she kept trying to make me feel guilty. It's too bad it had to be that way when she could really have enjoyed her last days."

They were in Virginia Beach for two years, during which time her mother was hospitalized three times with increasingly serious heart problems. After her third hospitalization, she was too sick for Flo to take care of her, so she was moved to a nursing home, where she died a month later. Even in the nursing home, Flo said, her mother seemed to blame her for her condition, and she actually stopped speaking to her daughter entirely. "I knew she was *choosing* not to speak to me," Flo said, "because she spoke to the doctors and nurses and to her other visitors."

Flo's first dream visit from her mother came just a week after her death. Flo prefaced her description of the dream by telling me that her mother had never had a formal education and that, toward the end of her life, they had spent a lot of time in the bathroom together as Flo helped her mother with her grooming. In the dream she and her mother were in a school bathroom, they were both carrying backpacks, and they hugged and kissed, very happy to see one another. Then her mother said, "I'm learning to speak French and German."

"It felt so good," Flo told me. "I felt that we'd had a reconciliation. Then I kept waiting to have more confirmation from her. I just wanted to know she was okay, so in my prayers I would ask for more confirmation."

Flo had a dear friend, Edith, who had also known her mother and who kept reassuring Flo, saying over and over, "Don't worry about her. I'm telling you, she's okay." But somehow that wasn't enough; she needed something more to assuage her guilt. It came seven months later, with a second dream and a dramatic manifestation. In this dream Flo's mother was standing behind a door. Flo couldn't see her, but she could hear her voice saying, "I can't do it, I just can't do it." Flo couldn't figure out what that meant, so she called a friend who was a psychic. Her friend told her that sometimes souls in transition, when they're passing over, don't have the energy to communicate and make a connection at that moment. "But, do you have a rosebush that's budding in your garden?" she asked. Flo did have a rosebush, and when she'd hung up, she went to look at it. It wasn't budding, and Flo said, "I was really, really disappointed. But then I turned around. My friend Edith had given my mother a chrysanthemum plant when she was in the nursing home, and she had it with her the whole time she was there. After she passed, I couldn't bear to part with it, so I brought it home with me. It looked like it was dead, but I couldn't bear the thought of throwing it away. Now I saw that it had seven buds on it. I thought that was amazing after what my psychic friend had told me. It was really a communication that she was okay.

"That happened in February. In April I planted it, and it grew to be three feet tall with huge yellow mums on it."

At that point, I had to interject. "Flo, it was a *mum* plant!"

"Oh, my God," Flo answered. "I never thought of that. Thank you for that insight." She then went on to tell me that it had lived for two years and then suddenly died for absolutely no reason.

"Well," I asked, "wasn't it two years that you spent with your mother in Virginia Beach?" I then went on to suggest that I thought the first dream had signified that Flo's mother was learning to speak a new language, to communicate with her in a new way. The plant was symbolic of their last two years together in the new house, the years during which her mother had been so angry. Its blooming so fully and beautifully and then dying, I told her, might signify that her mother was letting her know she had really lived fully during that time and was no longer angry with Flo.

The end of Flo's story is both happy and sad. Her friend Edith became sick sometime after her mother's death. Flo then became a caretaker for her as she had been for her mother. Edith died at two o'clock in the afternoon on Flo's mother's birthday. At four o'clock, Flo told me, she had a vision of Edith in a beautiful red dress with her arm around Flo's mother, saying, "I told you she was okay."

"I started to laugh and cry at the same time," Flo said. "It felt so good. It was so obvious to me that they were both okay."

Flo didn't really have any reason to feel guilty; she'd done everything she possibly could for her mother while she lived. Because her mother seemed unable to understand that, however, her daughter needed to know that she was okay. No amount of reassurance from anyone else, including her dearest friend, could provide that. It was only through transcommunication that she was able fully to believe in her heart that it was true.

Sometimes It's Easier to Communicate After Death

Even though Flo's mother stopped talking to her in the end, they'd had a long history of close communication before that. Unfortunately, some of us, like Angie and Ariel, both of whom we met earlier in this chapter, do not have such a history. Angie, for example, had been bewildered by her grandfather's lying about her behavior and had not been able to question him about his reasons for treating her so badly. Ariel could not tell her father, the rabbi, how neglected by him she'd felt all her life. Others do communicate, but only on the most superficial level, as was the case for Isis and her father.

"I was angry when my father died," she told me. "Not at him, but at his leaving me. I was angry around the house, just walking around full of anger. One day I walked into the living room, where we have a big picture window with a bird feeder outside, and in the bird feeder I saw a big blackbird with a red breast. It was a very Spanish-looking bird, and my father was Spanish. There was a clear film around the bird, and I was able to see through it. I'd never seen that bird before, even though I'm a very serious bird-watcher. I was certain it was my father and that he was telling me not to be so angry. I didn't have to be in such great distress.

"That helped me to calm down, even though it took me a while to accept his death. After that experience, I kept calling him, saying, 'I want to see you again,' almost as if I were pestering him. One week later I saw this image with a filmy outline. I could see him, but this time he just looked scary, as if he were scaring me away. After that I just decided not to call him anymore. I felt his message to me was that I was supposed to let go, for me to realize I had to let it be and let *him* be, and that I had to stop saying to him, 'Where are you? Can I see you?' "

At that point in her story, Isis explained that she'd never had the connection with her father she wished she'd had, that she couldn't relate to him as she would have wanted. It's not that they weren't close or didn't talk to one another; it was simply that whenever she tried to have a serious or meaningful conversation with him, her father would begin to lecture rather than really listening to what she had to say. I suggested that it sounded to me as if she were still seeking the connection with him that she never had in life. She agreed that was probably true. At that point, nevertheless, she did stop trying to reach him.

Five years after that, when she was nine months pregnant, Isis had a terrible argument with her aunt. Her aunt was demanding that Isis take care of her, and Isis, at that point in her life, simply wasn't able to do so. She couldn't understand how her aunt could have made such a demand. Yet she also felt as if she must be a horrible person for refusing. In the midst of her inner turmoil, her father appeared to her and said, "I love you so much. You're my favorite child."

"It came out of the blue," Isis said. "I instantaneously felt incredible joy and peace. He was able to be there in such a powerful way. Since that time, there have been many other things that have happened that let me know he's connecting with me. He continues to be a source of comfort for me, and there are many times when he surprises me with this."

"So," I said, "although you were no longer asking him, he began to come through for you, and you've finally established the connection you wanted to have with him throughout your life."

"I never thought of it that way," Isis replied, "but, yes, I have the connection with him now that I always wanted. It came after he died. I had a craving for a heart-to-heart friendship with him where it would be comfortable for us to just talk. Instead of that, many times when we were together, there were those long cold silences. I didn't know what to say. I didn't know what to talk about. There was light conversation, like, 'How are you?' but nothing with depth or warmth."

Isis's lack of communication with her father in life wasn't either his fault or hers; they just never seemed to be on the same wavelength at the same time. His afterlife connections provided her with confirmation that he had understood what was missing in their relationship. They allowed her to feel loved, and as a result she's been able to reach out and speak to him from her heart. She now knows what to say and trusts the validity of his response.

As I've said from the beginning, sometimes the signs we receive from our loved ones in spirit are sent in a kind of Morse code. What helps us to interpret them is trusting our guts, bypassing our critical faculties, and accepting what the subconscious tells us as true. It's useful to note the ways Isis interpreted those first two signs he sent her. In the first, she interpreted the bird as "Spanish-looking," and in the second she felt that it was "scary." Flo knew that the flowering mum plant was a sign of her mother's forgiveness. And remember Michele, whom we met back in chapter 4? She interpreted the branch that crashed to the ground when a bird took flight as her father's validation of the decision she was making about her life.

Each of these people got something meaningful, powerful, and transforming from the signs they received. Yet, in the course of our conversations, I was able to show them that there was more to the messages than they'd been able to see. The impact of your connection can be so emotionally consuming in the moment that you may not immediately be able to recognize all the layers of its meaning. Give yourself some time, then revisit the message with a more objective eye.

To decipher your spiritual Morse code, consider the cathected objects that might have a special meaning for you or your loved one. Consider whether the sign occurred on a significant occasion such as a birthday or anniversary—either yours or that of your loved one. Consider the time involved—either the length of time that has elapsed since his or her death or the timing of the sign's arrival. Say the name of the sign out loud. What does it sound like? It might be something that sounds like the name of the person, the way heron sounds like Helen, or it might, as in Flo's case, be a mum plant. Being able to look at the symbols on this basic, literal level can be amazingly helpful because the subconscious is extremely literal in its interpretations of what it perceives. That is a key aspect of deciphering dreams. It can also be the key to deciphering your messages from the world of spirit.

Healing Relationships with the Living

As you've seen, those in spirit can reach out to us to make the connections we were never able to establish with them in life. In addition, they can also help us to facilitate and heal the relationships we have with those who are still living. Gabrielle's father did that when he sent Spooky, the kitten, to help her find a way to be closer to and spend time with her mother.

Sara, whose father had assured her of his continuing presence first by shaking her awake and then by acknowledging her anger, also came through to help her deal with her mother. Following that original validation, she's been able to continue talking to him and receiving answers when she needs them. At one point she was having a difficult time coping with the demands her mother was making both on her time and on her emotional resources. She said aloud in her exasperation, "Daddy, what should I do about Mom?" The response she heard was typical but right to the point: "She's a pain in the ass, but put up with her and don't take her so seriously." Just knowing he was there and that he understood her frustration has helped Sara to let her mother's annoying behavior roll off her back.

Since Sara's relationship with her father had at times been rocky in life, I asked why she thought that she could now ask for and receive his help. Her response was, "Well, I believe he's now free. I ask him instead of God because God is overlaid with so many images and seems so distant. My father is like a funnel to God."

Eileen, another patient of mine, really became stuck, both emotionally and literally, with her mother after the death of her father. An only child, Eileen had been very close to him and knew how much he had done to take care of her mother. After he died, she felt tremendously responsible for taking over those duties.

The lease on her apartment was up, and she'd been planning to move anyway, so she decided she'd temporarily move in with her mother to try to see her through the first months after her father's death, which she knew would be difficult.

When she was cleaning out her apartment, three or four weeks after his death, in preparation for the move, she came upon a birthday card he had sent. She remarked to me that it was probably the only card her father had ever sent her in his life. Normally it was her mother who chose and sent cards, signing both their names. This one, however, was signed in his own handwriting, and its sentiments expressed everything she would have wanted her father to know *she* felt about *him*—you know I love you; you're so special to me, and so on. It was just perfect, she said. "I was weeping as I read it because the connection felt so strong. I was sure he knew how much I really loved him." She also felt that finding that card validated the decision she'd made to move in with her mother.

Six months later she was still living there, trying to extricate herself from what was becoming an ever-more-difficult situation. Her mother was becoming less able to take care of herself, leaving lights on, trying to eat frozen food directly from the refrigerator, and becoming more and more dependent on her daughter.

One day when she felt she was really at the end of her rope, Eileen drove to the cemetery, trying to work out in her mind how she was going to manage to move out and move on and how she'd be able to get her mother the professional caregiving help she so clearly needed. She was puttering around her father's grave, weeding, cleaning up the grounds, trying to get some sense of peace for herself, and talking aloud to her father as she did so, saying, "Daddy, I love her, but I really need to take care of myself."

When she got back in her car and turned on the radio, the first song she heard was "You Can Go Your Own Way," by Fleetwood Mac. Eileen took that as a sign that her father was giving her permission to go, and that understanding was what she truly needed to alleviate her guilt.

Sometime later, she'd rented an apartment but hadn't yet moved out of her mother's house. Eileen told me then that she was truly at her wit's end, about ready to have a breakdown. "Mom was still refusing to meet the caretaker I'd put in place, and I felt as if I were going to war. It was going to be me or my mother." She was working late in her office, crying and listening to music on her computer, when once again she heard "You Can Go Your Own Way." Again she felt it was a sign from her father answering her in her distress and saying, "You have to be independent. You have to live your own life." She felt that her father was encouraging and supporting her and that the song was confirmation that she was on the right track. Eileen was able to use that connection as a tool for alleviating the guilt she felt about leaving her mother. She was finally able to work through her emotions and move into her own apartment, while her mother has been able to manage without her because of the professional caretaking Eileen had put into place.

Recovery from the pain of conflicted relationships as well as their renewal on a different plane take place, as we've seen, in many ways. The connections those in spirit are able to make both with and between their loved ones on earth can occur on many levels. Jonna Rae's husband, Paul, who sent her so many healing signs and messages after his death from melanoma, also found a way to heal the long-standing rift that had been keeping his mother and brother apart even while his spirit was still in transition.

When he knew the end of his long and painful illness was near, he went into a hospice, where he knew that, at the time he determined it was necessary, the doctors would administer the level of morphine that would alleviate his pain and ultimately cause his death. It was on the night before the day he'd decided he would voluntarily go into a morphine coma that Jonna Rae had a dream in which she learned that she wouldn't be with him at the time of his passing. Because she and Paul had been so open with one another all along, she felt that if this were meant to happen, she could be at peace with it. She was at his bedside virtually around the clock during that entire weekend, and on Monday morning she went home briefly to shower. While she was gone, Paul's mother and brother were in his room, together for the first time in twenty years. They were each holding one of his hands when he died, before Jonna Rae could return.

Clearly her dream had come true. "The sacredness of that transition was astounding," she told me. "He brought them together in his final breath." Jonna Rae found peace in the knowledge that she and her husband had already said all there was to say to one another. She believes that her absence at the time of his death has served a greater purpose.

Finding Emotional Freedom Through Transcommunication

Establishing or continuing contact with those in the afterlife can help to alleviate unresolved anger, as it did for Angie and Dolores; it can help to unburden you of guilt, as it did Wilma and Flo. It can ease your separation anxiety so that you are better able to take care of yourself, as Wilma and Eileen discovered.

When Karin, whose older sister, Ellen, you may remember, sent her a sign in the guise of a buyer for her apartment, she was transformed from a skeptic to a believer. In addition, the connection she made at that time also empowered her to begin taking care of herself rather than worrying constantly about putting other people's feelings first.

When her sister was dying, Karin had felt terribly guilty because even when she was so ill, Ellen had continued to be protective of her younger sister's needs. By way of illustration she told me of the time she'd been visiting in the hospital when a male friend of Ellen's was also there. Karin knew that Ellen was worried about the fact that she wasn't married—yet another manifestation, in Karin's mind, of the maternal role her sister had taken on. Now as they sat in that hospital room, Ellen said teasingly to her friend, "I think you should marry my sister. Come on, how can you deny a dying woman her wish?" Karin was flabbergasted. Even though she knew her sister wasn't entirely serious, those words indicated to her how much Ellen was still concerned about her well-being. "How could she be thinking of me at a time like that?" she asked me in bewilderment. Because of her guilt, after Ellen's death Karin was struggling with allowing herself to live and love happily.

Once she was convinced that her sister had sent her the buyer for her apartment, however, her belief in their ongoing connection was so powerful that it gave her the courage to ask her brother-in-law for one of her sister's skirts and a pair of earrings. She'd wanted to do that for some time, but hadn't been able to. "I just couldn't. I don't know why," she said.

When I probed further into the reason for her previous reticence, Karin told me, "Well, I had it in my mind that he'd let me know when he was giving away her things and ask me if I wanted anything. I felt funny that he'd be uncomfortable and not want to deal with going through her closet. Then all of a sudden I felt

I could ask him and that I could have some of her belongings." The afterlife connection she'd made and the signs she'd received through conscious contact were so strong that they told her it was okay to keep a part of her sister.

Her renewed sense of having her sister in her life enabled her, for the first time, to feel entitled to take care of herself and not worry about how everyone around her might feel. In addition, she has finally been able to stand up to her business partner and defend herself when necessary. In the past she had always been intimidated by narcissistic, controlling people, who reminded her of her mother. Whenever her partner had verbally attacked her, she'd remained quiet, trying to keep the peace. When she spoke out for the first time, she said, "It was wonderful. I felt completely entitled to defend myself. I felt no guilt and no worry that she wouldn't like me." When I asked how her sister had helped her to do that, she told me, "I felt her completely with me." Then she added, "It's something she would have done."

Clinically, one might say that Karin was identifying with and incorporating her sister's strength. While she certainly was doing that, there was something more going on in the process of her healing. The key lies in her very words: She "felt" her sister's strength was there with her. That feeling had been accomplished through the empowerment she received by initiating conscious contact.

Opening the Door to Invite Spiritual Healing

Everyone has his or her life in some way irrevocably altered from the time he or she loses a loved one. We all do what we can to heal ourselves, get over it, and survive. However, I think we can do much more than that. I believe that continued communication with a loved one in spirit can qualitatively alter and accelerate the healing process. As these stories have illustrated, such communication can help you to move beyond surviving to recovering your well-being and even transforming your life.

I realize, nevertheless, that not everyone will be immediately ready to initiate conscious contact. The exercise in chapter 6 that I've called "Accentuate the Positive" is one tool I use to help my patients find their own power and transform negative feelings about their relationships without actually taking the leap that initiating conscious contact would require.

Role-playing is a tool that therapists have developed and use to help people gain insight into and transform relationships with the departed. I believe it is also a tool we can use to open ourselves up to the possibility of actual transcommunication. It can help you to recognize, identify, and get in touch with emotions you may have been unaware of carrying around. One function of psychotherapy is to help you bring up and release psychic energy. With role-playing, you can do that for yourself.

People have different ways of talking about negative emotions. Role-playing helps you to become more at ease with owning and giving voice to those emotions. Imagining the other person's response helps you to empathize with what his or her own issues might have been. Gaining that understanding enables you in turn to arrive at a level of acceptance you might never otherwise have achieved.

I call the script that follows "A Mother-Daughter Dialogue." I suggest that, if you're not yet ready to engage in transcommunication, you use it as a prototype for the kind of conversation you would ideally like to have with your loved one in spirit. The key to succeeding with this exercise is to be totally honest both in communicating your own feelings and in putting yourself in the place of your departed so that you can express his or her point of view as well. Ignore that little policeman in your head who will try to censor your thoughts and feelings. Go with your gut and speak from your heart.

A Mother-Daughter Dialogue

D: I'm still trying to please you. Can you release me now?

M: I'm not sure.

D: What do you need from me in order to free me?

M: Your understanding.

D: About what?

M: That I tried to be the perfect mother, and that that's why I failed you.

D: You tried to get me to be perfect.

M: I was conditioned to be perfect and to raise perfect children.

D: I do understand, but it's hard to let go of my anger.

M: Do you remember your grandmother?

D: Yes. You had a troubled relationship, and I was always nervous around her.

M: I continued her legacy. She did to me what I did to you, and, like you, I resented her when I got older.

D: So why couldn't you stop? Why did you continue her legacy?

M: I had no idea that I was repeating the past with you. I wasn't awake; I was operating on automatic pilot.

D: I wish you'd woken up!

M: I'm sorry. I couldn't. I was in too much pain. My mother made me feel worthless, and the only way I could succeed in her eyes and my own was to produce a perfect child.

D: I remember how hard life seemed for you, under that veneer of competence and happiness.

M: You knew the truth about me, but it didn't help you then. You couldn't use the information because you were too hurt and too dependent. But you can use it now, and I can help you now.

D: You can?

M: My heart and spirit are finally free. I'm finally free to help you, to be the mother I couldn't be when I was suffering.

D: You've been gone for a while. I wish you'd told me this sooner.

M: I guess I needed to know you understood first.

D: You have my understanding now.

M: Yes, I have it now. And I can release you so that you can be free and whole, with all your human frailties, all your problems, and all your gifts. You have my blessing forever.

I know from experience how difficult it is to recover from the devastating loss of a loved one. I also have experienced firsthand how much transcommunication can promote that recovery. I encourage you, therefore, with all the power of persuasion I can muster, to use these and whatever other tools you have available to cope. Only you can create the openness in yourself that will allow you to put out the welcome mat and ask your loved one in spirit for his or her guidance, support, love, and ongoing contact.

As you've seen, you can continue to reconcile conflict and alter your relationships with loved ones after death, especially when they have left a residue of bad feeling behind. In this way, although you can't change your past, you can change your future.

8.

Discovery and Transformation in the Here and Now

The only things that count in life are the imprints of love which we leave behind us after we are gone.

—ALBERT SCHWEITZER

Death is a point of departure, but it is also a point of origin. It entails the loss of your loved one and your departure from life the way you knew it to be. In order to heal, you must be willing to grow and in some way begin your life anew. Painful as this process may be, it also offers you the opportunity to set out in a new direction.

My mother's passing changed the way I view death and the way I practice psychotherapy. It also altered the nature of my self-help writing. Grief often propels people onto a path they'd never otherwise have considered taking. Carolee, for example, kept her brothers' spirits alive after the World Trade Center disaster by establishing a fund to help victims' families. Other people may become involved with some kind of activity that's related to the way their loved one died. Those who have lost someone to a particular disease might become involved in raising money to fund research or in organizing a support group. After her husband died of colon cancer, Katie Couric became a tireless advocate for testing and early detection of the disease. Those whose loved ones have died as a result of violence often become victims' advocates or activists for gun control. Thus one can turn a painful negative experience into something that is healing and life-enhancing.

Take John Walsh, for example. When his son Adam was abducted and murdered in 1981, Walsh was a partner in a hotel management firm in Hollywood, Florida. As a result of the tragedy he and his wife experienced, they became advocates for missing and exploited children. Their far-reaching efforts were instrumental in the passage of the Missing Children Act of 1982 and the Missing Children's Assistance Act of 1984. Walsh is now known to all of us as the host of *America's Most Wanted* and has been honored by law-enforcement officials around the country.

His is an extreme case, but it is far from unique. It's not unusual for people to find that after a loved one has died, their life moves in a new direction, often one they had never even contemplated. Many of those people attribute these changes to something or someone the deceased has sent their way. I'm no longer surprised—in fact, I've come to expect it—when people tell me they've met someone new or a new opportunity has dropped into their lap after the death of a loved one. To me, these occurrences are proof that their loved one in spirit is a continuing presence as well as a driving force in their life.

Certainly, since my mother's death, many new people have crossed my path. It seems that each time I describe my experiences or explain the subject of this book to someone, he or she knows at least one other person I simply "have to talk to." Many of them have told me that my contacting them has been a small miracle because they'd been anxious to share their story but hadn't yet found a way to do so.

My mother, as I've said, was always my greatest supporter. It's my belief that she's supporting me still. More than two years ago, when I hadn't yet decided whether or not to write about her death and our afterlife connection, I was writing to her in my journal and received this response: "The door that's going to open is the book on me, and it's the change you need to make to get the information out." I believe she's been helping not only me but also those whom I've met along the way to get the information out.

Triumph from Tragedy—A Life Transformed

One person whom I met rather late in this journey has told me a story of such transformation that he referred to it as a gift that saved his life.

Rob met Tracy in 1985 when they were both working at the same bookshop in Greenwich Village, and they immediately became friends and soul mates. In a memorial to her, he spoke of her thus: ". . . one of the dearest, sweetest people I have ever known or will ever know . . . I will always remember her beautiful smile and her wonderful laugh. She will always live in my heart, and no one can ever take that away from me."

Tracy died in the World Trade Center on September 11, 2001, changing Rob's life forever. The first time he went to Ground Zero was late that October, and he described that initial visit as "emotionally and physically devastating." Nevertheless, in November he went back with another of Tracy's friends. On that occasion he posted his memorial on one of the many makeshift message boards that had been erected near the site. "It was raining lightly," he said, "and I was crying. We were walking along, remembering Tracy, when suddenly my tears stopped. At the moment I realized I was no longer crying, my friend and I noticed that the rain stopped as well. We both knew it was a sign she was with us." That experience became the basis for a poem Rob wrote for Tracy, entitled "Angel Above," which has now been printed in several memorial books and published on the World Wide Web. One poignant verse reads:

> Loved ones write their own
> Words of sorrow and grief
> On a huge makeshift sheet
> I struggle through my tears
> To tell you those precious words
> I couldn't tell you
> When you were here
> In this life
> Now the rain and the tears
> Have both left together
> And the sun peeks
> Through the clouds
> Now I am so confident
> There's an Angel watching over us.

The poem alone has brought him into contact with people around the world who have been touched by his words and have written or sent e-mails telling him how moving they found it. A fourteen-year-old eighth grader in Missouri used the poem to win fourth place in her school poetry-reading contest. It's been read at memorial services and in churches from Edmonton, Canada, to Shreveport, Louisiana. Rob is a stockbroker, not a writer, but he felt compelled to memorialize his friend and to make certain she would be remembered. As he put it, "I've connected people to her who would never otherwise have had the chance to get to know her. That's the greatest gift for me." Yet even before all these people and events came into his life, Tracy made sure that Rob knew she was concerned and watching out for him.

Rob told me that, shortly after that November visit to Ground Zero, he made a decision. "I would be forty in January. I was very low both mentally and spiritually, and I decided not to celebrate my birthday. There was nothing to celebrate, and I would just let it go. The very next day my parents called to ask what I wanted to do for my birthday, and I told them 'nothing.' The only other person I'd said that to was a friend, Stephanie, who lives in England and to whom I'd sent an e-mail. A day or two later I received an e-mail back with the ominous heading 'Rob, you're going to think I've lost my mind, but . . .' And then in the body of the message, 'Something extraordinary is going on. I need to talk to you.'

"When I called her later that day, she told me an amazing story. She was being contacted by a spirit, she said. She'd feel a tapping on her shoulder, as if the spirit were trying to get her attention. That in itself was astounding to me because Stephanie is an extremely sensible, down-to-earth English housewife, not someone who had ever indicated that she was involved with any kind of spiritual or psychic phenomena. But what she went on to say was more astounding still. 'I've been getting messages,' she told me, 'visions of spirit, and—you're not going to believe this, but all these messages are for you!'

"When I heard that, cold chills ran down my spine. 'Have you seen the spirit?' I asked. 'What does it look like?'

" 'It's a woman with dark hair and dark eyes. She's almost always happy and laughing, and she cares about you.'

" 'Oh, my God,' I said. 'It's Tracy!' But how had Tracy found my friend in England? I determined that her spirit had been in the room with me when I was speaking to my parents. Then, when I sent the e-mail to Stephanie, Tracy knew she was the person to contact. Tracy had always been a 'party person,' and her own fortieth birthday had been the occasion for a really big celebration. So when she heard I'd decided not to celebrate mine, I think she decided it was time to take action. Stephanie told me that the spirit had conveyed to her that I'd be making a really big mistake not to celebrate. She also kept showing Stephanie red roses. When I heard that, I almost dropped the phone because I'd gone to Tracy's apartment and left red roses on six different occasions. Now she was coming through with a clear sign that told me she was giving them back to me.

"Several days later I called Stephanie back to let her know that since Tracy had gone to so much trouble, I felt I had to celebrate my birthday after all. Before I could get the words out, however, Stephanie said, 'Wait, I'm having a vision. I can see her face. What were you going to tell me?' 'I'm celebrating my birthday,' I said. 'Oh, my God,' came Stephanie's response. 'She's so happy. She's giving me thumbs-up. She's crying tears of joy.' I was so shook up. I couldn't believe this was happening."

Tracy was with Rob at his party, too. Just as everyone was about to sing "Happy Birthday," he stopped them. When the room was quiet, he announced that there was someone he wanted to acknowledge, a dear friend who couldn't be there but who was probably responsible for his having the party. He said he just couldn't let the day go by without acknowledging her. The next day, however, he had a new e-mail from Stephanie. This one was headed "You're not going to like this, but. . . ." Tracy had come to Stephanie that morning and told her she was upset with Rob for mentioning her on what should have been this day.

"I felt bad about that," he said. "So I took this beautiful picture of her that someone had given to me, and I put it on my bed and talked to her, explaining why I did that. I know she understood, and it made me feel much better."

These are just a few of the more extraordinary ways Tracy has made her continuing presence known to Rob, and just a few of the remarkable people and events who have come into his life since she died. He calls this transformation "a story of hope, a validation that there are angels and spirits around us." The last time I heard from him was just a few weeks before writing this. He told me he was trying to move forward with his life. "I know this will be difficult, but it is something I have to do. I am so proud of everything I have done for Tracy, and I know she is too. The poem and memorial are the proudest accomplishments of my life. But I feel like she is telling me to move on now."

Knowing she's still with him in spirit has been an essential element of Rob's healing process. Equally amazing are the ways in which his life has changed. He's become acquainted with people he never would have met, his words have touched hearts in ways he couldn't have imagined, and he's now aware of a spiritual realm he had never considered before that terrible and transforming day.

Sara, whose afterlife connections with her father I've already discussed, also found her life changed and made a new friend as the result of meeting a World Trade Center victim.

Sara's father had been ill for some time before he died. At one point he was in a coma, and her mother was unable to come to a decision about whether or not to take him off life support. Seeing her wrestle with this difficult decision, the doctors suggested that she ask Sara, who said, "Absolutely not." Sara went into her father's room that evening and sang spiritual songs to him throughout the night. Later, he came out of the coma, and he lived two more years. "I don't take responsibility for this miracle," Sara told me. "Rather I recognize that I was able to be the spiritual vessel that made it possible."

Sara had always known she had a lovely singing voice, but after that night she came to feel that her voice was truly a gift. That feeling was validated sometime later when she was singing in church one day and a man in the pew behind hers stopped her on the way out to say, "You sing like an angel." The remark prompted Sara's husband to suggest that she take lessons, which, in turn, has led to her devoting much more time to her singing, even giving public performances. The gentleman in church whose remark precipitated what has turned out to be a pivotal change in Sara's life was David Alger, the well-known Wall Street veteran and fund manager who died tragically in the World Trade Center.

The day after the tragedy, Sara says, she felt compelled to call Alger's wife to tell her what a gift her husband had given her. "I felt that I just needed to connect with her," Sara told me. They've now become friends. Sara believes that Mr. Alger's spirit is still with her and that she's supposed to be looking out for his wife.

Chance Meetings or Afterlife Assistance?

Very often, it seems, when a loved one dies, a new relationship is born. Equally often, people who find themselves making these unexpected connections in unusual ways are aware that someone in spirit has facilitated what would otherwise appear to be simply a quirky and offbeat chance encounter—what they call in the movie business "meeting cute." I had to smile when I read an article in the *New York Times* (July 25, 2002) about a young woman who moved back into her mother's apartment after the death of her father. She'd already met the young lawyer who lived down the hall from her mom and had written him off as "the frat boy from hell." Now, however, he sent her an extremely sensitive sympathy note that caused her to reassess him. They started seeing one another, and one night, in what the *Times* termed "a scene worthy of *Seinfeld*," the woman's mother got up in the middle of the night to find their neighbor hiding in one of her closets. Apparently he'd been with her daughter and was making a desperate attempt to prevent her from seeing him in the apartment. "After my mother kicked him out," the woman is quoted as saying, "I grabbed my pillow and my blanket and walked down the hall. We've been together ever since."

The young lawyer down the hall turned out to be Mr. Right after all. If this young woman's father hadn't died, however, she'd never have moved back into her parents' apartment. She'd never have had the opportunity to change her mind about him. I believe that her father in spirit had something to do with engineering that "chance encounter."

Maggie is a patient whose story typifies just this sort of not-really-by-chance meeting. Maggie is an attorney and an extremely youthful-looking woman. She came to me originally because she'd been dating Ed, a man twenty years her junior, who was now ending their relationship. Their breakup was devastating to her. In the course of her treatment and in working through her feelings, she began to talk about her father, who had been a successful and well-known architect. They'd had a very close relationship, and he'd been loving and supportive throughout her life. His work took him all over the world, and Maggie often traveled with him. After his death she had married a man twenty years older than she who eventually became emotionally abusive. It was after that marriage ended that she met and became involved with the man who was twenty years her junior.

I was struck by the symmetry and juxtaposition of those two relationships. In our sessions we began to explore what unfinished business Maggie might still have had to deal with. In time she came to understand that she had never really recovered from her father's death and that both these relationships had been efforts to regain what was most important about the relationship she had lost. In her marriage she was looking for the security and stability of the father she had known as a little girl. Then, when that marriage became too stifling, she once again attempted to deal with her unmet needs by becoming involved with Ed. In him she felt she had found a playmate with whom she was able to recapture the free-spirited aspect of the relationship she'd had with her father. Ed shared her excitement about traveling and discovering new places. Together they traveled the world, from Disneyland to Hong Kong, having a great deal of fun. The profound sense of loss she experienced following the breakup of that relationship is what had brought to light all the grief she'd been burying since her father died.

Having determined that she would be open to the concept, I discussed conscious contact with her, explained how important and healing it could be, and suggested that she try to connect with her father. I told her she could let him know how much she missed him and ask him for some protection at this vulnerable period in her life.

After our conversation she did initiate conscious contact by asking her father for a sign. Two weeks later she came to our session a changed woman. "I've met the most amazing man," she exclaimed as soon as I'd closed my office door. "And you won't believe how it happened! I was sitting on the subway going downtown and wearing my hat with the American flag on it. This guy was right across the aisle from me wearing an American flag tie. He noticed my hat and started talking to me. We struck up an interesting conversation that continued until I reached my stop. I told him my first name, that I was a lawyer, and I mentioned the firm where I worked. As I was getting off, I told him how much I'd enjoyed talking with him. Well, can you believe it—he tracked me down at work and called me. Turns out he's a restaurant critic, and he's been wining and dining me ever since. We had an instantaneous connection, and it's amazing how much we have in common. He combines the best of what I loved about my husband and my boyfriend. I just know my father sent him to me after you suggested I ask for his help."

His coming through validated for Maggie his continuing presence in her life. "It was such a remarkably healing experience," she told me afterwards. "I knew my father was there and that I didn't have to keep on looking for him in other men."

Our loved ones can put people in our path who will change our lives for the better. Before that could happen, however, Maggie needed to accept the possibility that her father could still be a part of her life. Therapeutically, she also needed to understand that she had been trying to replace him by entering relationships with emotionally unavailable men. Once she was able to see both those things, she was open to starting a new and healthier relationship when it came her way.

Maggie isn't the only one of my patients who's met men she believes were sent by her father. Nancy, a lovely-looking woman with a successful career as a publicist, has also had that experience on more than one occasion.

The first of these meetings occurred on her father's birthday. Nancy had called her mother to see how she was feeling because she knew it would be a difficult day for her. Her mother was not doing well and asked Nancy to buy a candle they could light to celebrate his life. On her way into the shop near her apartment on the upper West Side of Manhattan, she noticed an attractive man standing outside. She says that she felt an immediate connection with him. So when she came out with her purchase and he was still there, she did something totally out of character for her. "I just walked up and introduced myself. He told me his name was Jordan, and we began to chat." They wound up walking together for about two hours. During the course of their conversation, it turned out that Jordan was a television personality who believed that Nancy had approached him because she recognized him, though actually she had no idea who he was. Soon they developed a powerful bond and became close friends.

Before her father died, Nancy had worked for him in his business. She had never felt that he thought her work was good enough and had spent much of her adulthood trying to prove herself to him. After connecting with Jordan, however, she became his publicist. Because they met on her father's birthday, she believes he was sent by her dad as a way of letting her know that he thought she was up to the job—something he was never able to make her feel during his lifetime.

After her father's death Nancy's mother had given her back a pair of cuff links that she'd given him for his birthday twenty years before. Now, because they'd met on her father's birthday, and because of the "father connection" she believes they share, she has given the cuff links to Jordan as a gesture of their bond and of her sense that a part of her father is still alive in him.

Nancy also believes that her father sent another man her way. She was at Ground Zero one day, gazing at the site and reliving her own father's death in her mind, when a fellow visitor struck up a conversation with her. She began to talk about her father, partly because she'd just been thinking about him and partly because, as she told me, talking about her father is a way to bring him to life. That chance meeting also turned into a long-term business relationship as Nancy began to work for this second man as well. Again, she believes it was her father who sent him her way.

"I'm not blessed to have my dad passed away," she said, "but I'm blessed that he brought these two men into my life."

Love Begets Love—New Relationships Sent by Our Guardian Angels

I believe our loved ones in spirit truly want us to be happy. One of the ways they can help to make their wish for us come true is to send us someone to love. That said, we should not try to make this new person a replacement for our lost loved one. Attempting to do that, as we've seen with Maggie, is a way to repress our grief and remain stuck in the past rather than to truly heal from our loss. What our loved ones do want is for us to live a rich, full life, which might mean our entering into a new and fulfilling relationship.

Blossom is very much aware of her father's role in helping her to meet the man who became her husband. In November there had been a fire at the swim club Blossom belonged to on Long Island. Her cabana had burned to the ground, and she'd had many phone conversations with the insurance adjuster concerning her claim. In the course of their several conversations, Blossom found him interesting and thought she would like to meet him, but because she got the sense that he was involved in a relationship, she never brought up the possibility.

The following February she lost her father, who had been suffering from heart disease. Just a week later she and a friend had planned to drive from their homes on the East End of Long Island to attend a singles weekend at a Catskills resort. The weather reports, however, were predicting bad storms, so the two women decided not to drive into the mountains but to remain on Long Island instead. On Saturday evening they set out for a restaurant on the opposite shore, where they thought the weather wouldn't be as bad. When they got there, the place was completely deserted. By eleven-thirty they were alone at the bar, having a drink, and the snow had really begun to come down. Suddenly the door opened, and a single man walked in. Naturally enough, since they all seemed to be travelers seeking shelter from the storm, he sat down near them and offered to buy them a drink. He told them his name was Morty and asked theirs. When Blossom responded, he said, "That's funny, I've just recently been doing some business with a woman named Blossom, and it's a rather unusual name."

"Oh, my God!" she exclaimed. "You're *that* Morty!"

They quickly fell into an animated conversation, and later that evening Blossom told her friend, "I'm going to marry that man."

Intuitively, Blossom had been right. When they first spoke on the phone, Morty had been involved with someone, but that relationship now became a thing of the past. Blossom did indeed marry him, and they are now happily husband and wife. "I felt like my daddy had sent him down to me," Blossom told me. "Morty's just like him—same sense of humor, same height, same general physical appearance."

Morty can never replace Blossom's father, nor would he want to. Their bond, however, is strengthened by her conviction that her daddy did, in some way, put Morty in her path. To Blossom this means not only that her father is aware of and happy about her marriage but also that he remains very much a part of her life.

It's interesting to note that Blossom and her friend had canceled previous plans and made a definite choice to drive all the way across Long Island to that particular restaurant on the night she and Morty met, and that Blossom has always believed it was her father's spirit that drove her to that meeting.

Entrances and Exits—Two Ways to Move On

Very often, I have found, a death is balanced by the arrival of a new life. This was literally true in the case of Callie, whose next-older sibling had died just a month before her birth and whose mother had told her, "You're my special angel. Without you I wouldn't have survived your brother's death." It was also true of my friend Josie, whose daughter was born following a very difficult delivery just three weeks after her sister died. Josie has always believed that her sister's death somehow made it possible for her baby to live.

For Brian, a karate teacher from Colorado, the birth was more symbolic than literal. Ten years ago Brian was teaching an accredited karate class at a local college. He was very attracted to one of his female students, but because he had made it a rule never to date anyone in his classes, he didn't ask her out until the course was over. He did call her then, and they went out for dinner. It turned out that the woman, whose name was Jeannie, was married but having a difficult time with her husband, who, she'd discovered, had been having an extramarital affair. Brian couldn't be certain that her interest in him wasn't really based on her desire to take revenge on her husband, but they nevertheless began a relationship that eventually led to her leaving the marriage. She and Brian were together for more than a year, but Jeannie was never divorced.

Brian was concerned that she might become pregnant during this time, but Jeannie assured him that she very much wanted to have a baby. Although she already had an eleven-year-old daughter from a previous marriage, whom Brian had met when she took one of his classes, she and her present husband had never been able to conceive and had spent thousands of dollars on fertility treatment. When Jeannie did become pregnant she was very open about telling people it was Brian's baby, and Brian was thrilled. He was thirty-eight years old at the time, had never been married, and finally felt ready to make the commitment.

Then, six months into her pregnancy, he became aware that Jeannie seemed to be pulling away from him, acting cold and distant. Brian, the typical male, attributed her behavior to hormones and mentally wrote it off. A month after that, however, Jeannie moved back in with her husband and announced that Brian wouldn't have any rights to see or be involved with his child.

He went to see an attorney and was prepared to fight her legally, but when she stopped talking to him altogether, he dropped the suit, hoping that she'd come around. That didn't happen, and two years later Jeannie and her husband moved with the two children to Texas. Brian never even saw a photograph of his daughter until she was five years old. Then, out of the blue, Jeannie sent him a Christmas card with a family photo on it.

Brian was overjoyed. The little girl, he said, looked exactly like him. Sadly, however, there was no further contact.

Both of Brian's parents, to whom he had been extremely close, died in the last two years within ten months of one another. They'd been married for fifty-three years, and Brian believes that his mother, who went after her husband, died of a broken heart.

Brian told me that just this past August a miracle occurred. Each year all the "Leos" at his gym hold a joint birthday party. This year, at four o'clock in the morning on the day of the party, which was also Brian's actual birthday, the telephone rang. He let his answering machine pick up and heard Jeannie's voice saying she'd been thinking about him and leaving a local telephone number. She and her family were back in Colorado for a visit. Brian phoned back and invited both Jeannie and her older daughter to the Leo party that day. The daughter, who is now a grown young woman, arrived first. She told Brian that his daughter, Courtney, now almost ten years old, was also there. Jeannie, she said, had told Courtney all about Brian, including the fact that he was her biological father and would be bringing her to the party.

Since then, Jeannie and her husband have moved back to Colorado so that Courtney could get to know her father and have him play a role in her life. "It's just amazing," Brian told me. "She looks just like me. She loves gymnastics. She's going to be in the junior Olympics, and she's learning karate.

"My mother always wanted a little girl and only had two boys. I really believe my parents helped to bring Courtney into my life. I took her to visit the house where I grew up, and she was just fascinated with my mother's bedroom. She went right in there and started looking in the drawers. Then she said that if we ever stayed in the house, she wanted to sleep in that room. I really felt that my mother was in that bedroom with us. It gave me the chills."

Brian is aware of his mother's spirit in his daughter. He believes his mother knows about their relationship and was somehow instrumental in making it happen. It's as if his daughter had been born to him for the first time, and her entrance into his life has changed its path forever, bringing him a kind of joy he would never otherwise have known.

Entrances and exits use the same doorways, so that sometimes an exit can also be the way to enter on a new and better path. Lynn discovered this with the help of a dream visit from her aunt. Lynn's relationship with her own mother had been troubled and often conflicted. As a result, her aunt became a kind of mother figure for her, phoning regularly to check on her niece and make sure that she was okay.

At the time of her aunt's dream visit, Lynn had been married a short time. She was pregnant, but her marriage was already falling apart. She and her husband were sleeping in separate rooms and barely speaking to one another.

In her dream, Lynn told me, she was at a wedding, and she was pregnant. Her aunt was also there, "wearing a beautiful green dress and dancing." Lynn was holding the hand of the baby she was carrying as if holding a new life, and she was showing the baby to her aunt.

"Oh, my God," her aunt said. "It's an emergency. We have to get her out of here right now. You have to get out."

To Lynn, her aunt's message was clear. She had to leave her husband and move on with her life. She'd been trying to hold on to the relationship for the sake of her child. "But," she said, "after that dream I knew she wanted to protect me. I felt she was watching over me. I know she's in my corner. I feel her presence, and that's very important. It gives me the strength to do what I know is right for me and my child."

What or Who Is Coming into Your Life?

It's easy enough to chalk up chance meetings or life-changing events to luck or coincidence. Yet if we're open to the power those in spirit can wield, it becomes possible for us to see how our loved ones might still be guiding, protecting, and looking out for us. That understanding can be both energizing and liberating. We may be more certain about the decisions we make for ourselves when we know they are spiritually guided by someone whom we love and whom we know has our best interests at heart. We feel less alone, less adrift. We can step out and move on with greater confidence when we know there's a guardian angel looking over our shoulder.

I truly encourage you, therefore, to consider who's come into your life in the wake of your loss. If you've met a new person and thought to yourself that he or she really reminds you of your mother or father, or if you've thought that your sister would really have loved your new beau, consider that your mother or father or sister might have sent that person your way, not as a replacement for their love, but as an extension of it—because they know he or she can bring you a new kind of love and happiness.

If your life has taken a turn you wouldn't have expected, and you feel your loved one in spirit would have approved of the choices you're making, consider that he or she might have been guiding those choices. My personal experience, as well as the experiences of those who've stories I've shared, has been that spiritual energy does exist, and that it flows two ways. If you are able to recognize the presence of that energy in your life, I believe it can give your life greater meaning because it is a testament to the fact that we are all part of a greater whole, a universe that lies beyond what the eye can see but that the heart and mind can grasp.

Learning to live with the loss of a loved one is an ongoing process. While you never get over it, you do get on with it. My hope is that sharing my story will help you get on with your own personal journey so that you, too, can experience comfort, peace of heart, and serenity of mind from your afterlife connection. As I've said, a primary purpose in my life has always been to "pass on" whatever it is I have been able to learn or discover that might be helpful to other people.

Just a year or so before she became ill, my mother began to keep a journal. When I was reading through her reflections not so long ago, I came upon these lines written on the next-to-last page:

When it's time to "go,"
all one can take
with him is
what he has given
away.

I'd always known that my mother had started me on this journey; however, when I saw her words, I realized that, remarkably, she'd brought me full circle as well. For she believed, as do I, that what you pass on lives on.

In one of the stars I shall be living,

In one of them I shall be laughing.

And so it will be as if all the stars were laughing

When you look at the sky at night.

—ANTOINE DE ST. EXUPÉRY, *The Little Prince*

Suggested Reading

Anderson, George, and Andrew Barone. *George Anderson's Lessons from the Light*. New York: G. P. Putnam's Sons, 1999.

Browne, Mary T. *Life After Death*. New York: Ivy Books, 1995.

Cameron, Julia. *The Artist's Way*. Los Angeles: J. P. Tarcher, 2002.

Edward, John. *One Last Time*. New York: Berkley Books, 1999.

———. *Crossing Over*. San Diego, Calif.: Jodere Group, 2001.

Gauld, Alan. *Mediumship and Survival*. London: Paladin Books, 1983.

Goldberg, Natalie. *Writing Down the Bones*. Boston: Shambala, 1986.

Goldsmith, Joel S. *A Parenthesis in Eternity*. San Francisco: HarperSanFrancisco, 1963.

Guggenheim, Bill, and Judy Guggenheim. *Hello From Heaven!* New York: Bantam Books, 1997.

Hamilton-Parker, Craig, with Jane Hamilton-Parker. *The Psychic Workbook*. London: Vermillion, 1995.

Harra, Carmen. *Everyday Karma*. New York: Ballantine Books, 2002.

Kravich, Sally Pansing. *Vibrant Living*. Los Angeles: SPK Publications, 2002.

LaGrand, Louis E. *After Death Communication*. St. Paul, Minn.: Llewellyn Publications, 1998

————. *Messages and Miracles*. St. Paul, Minn.: Llewellyn Publications, 1999.

Lawson, Lee. *Visitations from the Afterlife*. San Francisco: HarperSanFrancisco, 2000.

Levine, Stephen. *Guided Meditations, Explorations and Healings.* New York: Anchor Books, 1991.

Margolis, Char, with Victoria St. George. *Questions from Earth, Answers from Heaven*. New York: St. Martin's Press, 1999.

Martin, Joel, and Patricia Romanowski. *Love Beyond Life*. New York: Dell Publishing, 1998.

Moody, Raymond A., Jr., M.D. *Life After Life*. New York: Bantam Books, 1976.

Moody, Raymond A., Jr., M.D., with Paul Perry. *Reunions*. New York: Ivy Books, 1994.

Northrop, Suzane, with Kate McLoughlin. *The Séance*. New York: Dell Publishing, 1995.

Picardie, Justine. *Life and Love After Death*. New York: Riverhead, 2002.

Picardie, Ruth. *Before I Say Goodbye*. New York: Owl Books, 1997.

Richmond, Cynthia. *Dream Power*. New York: Fireside Press, 2001.

Rothschild, Joel. *Signals*. Novato, Calif.: New World Library, 2001.

Schwartz, Gary E., Ph.D., with William L. Simon. *The Afterlife Experiments*. New York: Pocket Books, 2002.

Sechrist, Elsie R. *Death Does Not Part Us*. New York: St. Martin's Paperbacks, 1999.

Smith, Susy. *The Afterlife Codes*. Charlottesville, Va.: Hampton Roads, 2000.

Spangler, David. *Everyday Miracles*. New York: Bantam Books, 1996.

Steinpach, Dr. Richard. *Why We Live After Death*. Gambier, Ohio: Grail Foundation Press, 1995.

Van Praagh, James. *Talking to Heaven*. New York: Signet, 1999.

Virtue, Doreen, Ph.D. *Angel Therapy.* Carson, Calif.: Hay House, 1997.

Von Franz, Marie-Louise. *On Dreams and Death.* Boston: Shambala, 1987.

Weiss, Brian, M.D. *Messages from the Masters.* New York: Warner Books, 2000.

Windsor, Joan. *Dreams and Healing.* New York: Dodd, Mead & Company, 1987.

Acknowledgments

The writing of this book, although at times painful, has ultimately been an experience of cosmic blessings because of the extraordinary people with whom I've had the good fortune to work.

I am forever indebted to my friend and former editor, Frances Jones. You encouraged me to share my very personal experience and pointed my writing in a new direction. As if that wasn't enough, you steered me into the immensely talented hands of Janis Vallely, my agent.

Janis, you have truly been the silver lining that emerged from my gray cloud of loss. Your belief, wisdom, intuitive literary knack, savvy guidance, and hand-holding support throughout this project have been invaluable. Thank you for being my lucky charm.

Others on my dream team are Toni Robino, Deborah Chiel, and Henry Dreher. Each of you made a substantive contribution during the early stages of this book. Thank you for getting the ball rolling.

Judy Kern, my collaborator, carried the ball across the finish line. You did a superb job of capturing the essence of my mother and bringing her spirit to life. Thank you for your golden touch. As my mother would say, "You're some terrific dame, and you sure know your stuff!"

And the captain of my dream team is my editor, Jane Rosenman.

My profound thanks for your prevailing vision of what this book should be. You inspired and enabled me to take it to new heights and to "pass it on." Ethan Friedman, you are the best.

I am also supremely appreciative of and grateful to my many dear friends, colleagues, patients, and acquaintances, including those individuals who have chosen to remain anonymous, for sharing their very poignant and touching experiences with me.

Thank you to Blossom and Marty Abrams, Emme and Phil Aronson, Dr. Dale Atkins, Jonna Rae Bartges, Dr. Jan Berlin, Elizabeth Cohen, Isis Cohen, Charlie and Peggy Cook, Carmen Harra, Sally Kravich, Dolores McCullough, Neal Padlovsky, Maria Papapetros, Wilma Parker, Cynthia Richmond, Flo Rizzo, John Snowdon and Judith Newman, and Laura Wynn.

My father and brother certainly knew the delight and joy of spending time with my mother.

So did my cousins Marta Kustas, Jonathan Pearlman, Marisa Wolpert, and Samantha Fetter; my in-laws, the Aprils and the Snowmans; and my family of cherished friends, Kathy Pomerantz, Louise DuArt, and Lesley Kaminsky. Thank you for your loving presence in my life.

A special thanks goes to my trusted colleague and sister of the heart, Dr. Josie Palleja. Your wisdom concerning the importance of the "aha" moment was vital to shaping this book, as was your insightful technical advice. You have literally stepped into my mother's shoes and continue to fill my life with your tender loving care. For that I will always treasure you.

And, of course, my husband and colleague, Marc Snowman. You saw me through my darkest hour in time. Then and now your steadfast love brightens my life and sustains me. I am eternally thankful, and I love you dearly.